AFTER GOD

AFTER GOD
THE FUTURE OF RELIGION

DON CUPITT

Weidenfeld & Nicolson
LONDON

First published in Great Britain in 1997
by Weidenfeld & Nicolson

Published in association with Basic Books,
a division of HarperCollins Publishers, Inc.

A CIP catalogue record for this book
is available from the British Library.

ISBN 0 297 81952 6

Printed and bound in Great Britain by
Butler & Tanner Ltd, Frome and London

CONTENTS

⹀INTRODUCTION

This book outlines a theory of the history, and the future, of religious meaning. I write it in response to the great cultural event that has dominated my life, and perhaps yours, too—namely, the revolutionary change in human consciousness and the collapse of religious meaning that has been taking place since the end of World War II.

In 1952 I left an English boarding school and entered Cambridge University to study Natural Sciences. Within weeks I had converted to Christianity, and in just under seven years I was ordained into the ministry of the Church of England.

The 1950s are generally and correctly remembered as the very last years of a fairly confident and secure mainline traditional religious consciousness and national identity. One reason for this is that after the war, the range of options was so narrow. A young person growing up might choose to be either a Christian or a humanist. After Hitler and Stalin, one militantly rejected modernizing atheistic humanism, and the utilitarian humanism of those who advocated a fully planned society was utterly soulless. To a whole generation of Britons, it seemed clear that we should opt for liberal Toryism and

Anglicanism, rather as our counterparts on the European mainland were voting Christian Democrat and in the United States were basking in the Eisenhower years.

The major intellectual challenges to religion of which we were aware at that time were associated with the names of figures like Freud, Sartre, Russell, and Ayer. We heard of and talked about the Verification Principle, which declared that beliefs were meaningless unless they could be tested against experience, but we were not badly rattled because our religious consciousness was very vivid. God, grace, eternal life, and the unchanging identity of one's immortal soul were completely real to us. We read the works of the mystics, especially the fourteenth-century mystics, with a sense of recognition. That was how it felt to *us*, too.

But the revolutionary forces that were to change all this were already stirring. The first of them was cheap mass travel and mass economic migration. As the politicians liquidated the old colonial empires, labor shortages in Europe began attracting large numbers of migrant workers from the Caribbean, from Africa, and from Asia, making Western countries more and more multiethnic and multifaith, and making us all acutely aware of the way religion is bound up with language and cultural identity. Genuinely monocultural states are now very much the exception. In multicultural states, religion is by no means always a force that makes for civil peace. On the contrary, it is a commonplace observation that around the world most wars are now civil wars, and that religious differences are a significant factor in most conflicts.

The second force was the changeover, already beginning, to a mass consumer society led by the media and the mysterious business of fashion. Intellectual interest in the late 1950s (for example, in Roland Barthes's *Mythologies*) was turning toward language, communication, display, packaging, signaling, style, image, and symbolic exchange. Strange: in the old religious consciousness, "identity" was something metaphysical; now it increasingly became simply a "corporate ID," not a substance but a sign. Reality itself was becoming only an effect, something conjured up within and by the motion of signs. The line between drama and documentary, reality and fiction, became blurred, and the daily absorption of media output began to take the place of prayer in people's lives.

In retrospect, I find it curious that in my late teens I would go for many weeks at a time without any contact at all with the media. Many people then kept in daily touch with God and the motion of God's Spirit, rather as one now keeps in touch with the Zeitgeist through the media. Writers such as John Updike and Umberto Eco have suggested that in modern, media-led culture, we have in effect a return of the Middle Ages: it used to be the Church that supplied everyone with an imaginary world in his or her own head; now the media do that job, with celebrity as the new sainthood.

Third, new scientific advances and new technologies were already developing fast in the 1950s: standard-model physical cosmology, molecular biology, computers, rockets and artificial satellites, medicine, and the helping professions. Thirty or forty years later, a single global technological civilization is rapidly establishing itself. From its point of view, religion increasingly looks like a troublesome survival from the past: a local and traditional way of symbolizing, enacting, and combatively asserting one's own distinctive ethnic identity, in the face of the threat of assimilation into the all-encompassing anonymity of the new global culture. Religion everywhere seems to be embattled, fighting a rearguard action that it must eventually lose.

It seems obvious now that the religious neoconservatism of the fifties was never destined to be more than a brief interlude. In the sixties, it was quickly swept away. How could the consciousness of God and of an umbilical, continuous connection with God have been so real so recently, and then have faded so completely?

The problem is not one for Christians alone. In the new high-rise postmodern cities of South and East Asia, the wipeout of tradition is breathtaking—and it is all happening without any obvious resistance or regret, and within a single lifetime. It is perhaps the most severe and sudden cultural rupture in the whole of human history.

The new global technological culture brings with it a very naturalistic cast of mind. The world is like a communications network. Everything is open, public, accessible, and all on one level. Nothing is deep, and nothing can be kept hidden for long. There is no secure privacy, either in one's soul or anywhere else: the world of signs is a flowing, one-level continuum with no outside and no secret places.

Nevertheless, people do claim that it is possible to preserve something of our traditional faith and values in these strange new conditions. Religion, we are promised, can or does survive (1) as values; or (2) within the private or domestic realm; or (3) within individual subjectivity; or (4) in the last resort, as a counterculture.

What these four answers have in common is the belief that some sphere of life *can* be fenced off and kept inviolate, sheltered from the corrosive effects of postmodernity. The presumption is that we can draw at least one clear line, between the world as it is and the world as it ought to be—or perhaps between the public and the private, between objectivity and subjectivity, or between the dominant culture and the counterculture. But postmodernity as a cultural condition has been constituted precisely by the erasure of these very distinctions. The public realm, the sea of meanings, is outsideless and endless: nothing is fixed; everything moves and shifts together. It engulfs everything, including values, private life, selfhood, and the counterculture. There is no way of hiving off a little cluster of meanings (absolutes, certainties, or fundamentals) and preserving them unchanged. On the contrary, as the long history of religious esotericism all too amply demonstrates, meanings and truths kept unchallenged and out of public view very quickly deteriorate into simple nonsense. To stay meaningful, a language has to remain in free circulation.

Of the four answers, the first, that *religion can survive as values*, is associated especially with those politicians of the Right who, being economic liberals, have been the keenest promoters of free trade, the abolition of exchange controls, and the like. Because they do not want to be seen openly risking our moral and religious values by allowing them to float on the global market like our economic values, they try to argue for extreme economic liberalization combined with social and moral conservatism. Economic values are to be what, and only what, the open market decides they are, but moral values are allegedly something entirely different, something to be accepted from tradition and conserved unaltered. In the United States politicians speak of family values or the American way, in Singapore they speak of Asian values, and in Britain of Victorian values—and, of course, such talk makes not a whit of difference to the actual fate of the values in question. Moral values live, and they swim or sink, in our daily public converse, exactly like and along with economic values. People on the Right are very illogical if they refuse to acknowledge that *everything* nowadays is beginning to float on a free global market—not only money and prices but also linguistic meanings, religious truths, and moral and aesthetic values.

The second answer, that *religion can survive in the private or domestic realm*, is perhaps most closely associated with the example of the long survival of Orthodox Jewry. But too much weight cannot be conceded to this example, partly because, during the long centuries of their exclusion from public life in Christendom, the Jews themselves recognized that the only way to keep their tradition alive was to keep their language alive by becoming extremely bookish, talkative, and intelligent, and partly because nowadays, under the even more severe pressures of postmodernity, the Orthodox freely admit that they are as much threatened with disappearance by assimilation as any other religious group. The special qualities that helped them to survive in the past are no longer sufficient.

The third answer, that *religion can survive as personal faith within the sphere of individual subjectivity*, stems especially from Luther and Kierkegaard, and from the way modern Christian existentialists such as Rudolf Bultmann set out to demythologize the Gospel. Luther made a distinction between the Faith which is believed (*fides quae creditur*) and faith *by* which it is believed (*fides qua creditur*). Kierkegaard, developing this idea with brilliant clarity, says that in principle the "what" that is believed can be resolved completely down into the "how" of believing it (for example, in the closing pages of the *Concluding Unscientific Postscript*, 1846). If one were to get *being* a Christian right, as a matter of the kind of self one is and the way one's life is oriented, it would be unnecessary to mention the objective content believed. It could fall away, no longer needed.

More recently, Rudolf Bultmann similarly demythologized the Christian Gospel down into the form of Christian existence. In 1980–84 I put forward, in "Christian non-realism" (the doctrine that religious beliefs ought not to be understood as stating supernatural facts, because their true function is simply to produce a way of life), yet another version of the same idea. It ran into two problems: it was difficult even for ordinary people, and therefore quite impossible for church leaders, to understand; and by 1984–85 I was coming to see that the human self can no longer bear the weight that this doctrine puts upon it. All our thinking depended on language. But language is formed, and words get their meaning, in the to-and-fro of our common and public life. So the inner world of thought cannot be the place where everything begins. What goes on in my head is in no way primary or ultimate, and it is not sealed off: I am only a local and wholly contingent secondary privatization of bits of the general cultural flux. We are all of us much *lighter* than we were taught to think of ourselves as being. A generation ago, selfhood was still seen as a difficult task, and the cause of deep ontological anxiety. But now we must learn to be mere happenstance, felicitous froth, carefree.

The fourth answer, that *religion and eternal values can survive in the form of a counterculture*, is associated especially with the various New Age cults, fundamentalisms, charismatic Christianity, and other movements that try to rebel against and escape from what Western culture has become. But it goes without saying that all such movements fail, whether they are led by Californian prophets or by popes and ayatollahs. In the new understanding of culture as a system of signs in motion, the world of symbolic meaning in which we live is an outsideless and unanchored floating continuum. All reactions against it must use its vocabulary and are therefore part of it, and will be engulfed by it. You can't really drop out. There is nowhere to drop out to. Your protest against the system remains part of the system.

The last supernaturalist illusion is the belief that we can find salvation by retreating into some fenced-off and privileged area: a personal spirituality, a local vocabulary, an ethnic group, a traditional certainty. Such a retreat was indeed very common in the past, but today its effects are pernicious. Cultural, national, and religious identities used to be constructed out of differences—divisions and exclusions. Every *we* always identified itself as being not-like-*them*. Philadelphia was always built on a firm foundation of xenophobia: thus, Jews defined themselves by the way they separated themselves from gentiles, and Christians similarly from Jews, and Muslims from Christians, with the long-term result that the more clearly any human group identifies itself, the more it sees itself as surrounded by enemies. It was your instinct and your duty to stay with your own kind. And since about the time of Hegel, every renewal and reaffirmation of group feeling and group identity has always been accompanied by an intensified animosity toward outsiders. The more identity you have, the more ethnocentric you are and the less you love foreigners. The more orthodox you are, the more you will develop a victim psychology.

To escape this danger, I shall propose that if we can't beat postmodernity, we should embrace it. I am proposing a very considerable redefinition of religion, a redefinition that (to adopt the Christian vocabulary) will bring religion closer to the Kingdom than to the Church, closer to the Sermon on the Mount than to any sort of orthodox theology, and will make it very short-termist in outlook. Unlike the secular theologies of the 1960s, it will "aestheticize" religion, in the sense that it sees religious living in terms of artistic practice and symbolic expression. As redefined here, religious life is an expressive, world-building activity through which we can get ourselves together and find a kind of posthumous, or retrospective, happiness.

In the meantime, the dictionary still defines *religion* in terms of supernatural belief. People are going to protest that nearly all human beings throughout history have lived enclosed within a magical and religious style of thinking and vision of the world. Humans have believed in a great range of invisible supernatural beings and powers, in heavens and hells, in gods and spirits and departed souls. If I am simply discarding all that, and yet still retaining the word *religion*, I've got a lot of explaining to do. Why did we have to come this way? Why did we have to trudge through all those millennia of supernatural belief and mythical thinking before we could come to the simple and obvious truth? Why has the education of the human race followed such a bizarre and circuitous route?

This question gives us our agenda. We need a philosophy of our own religious history that will help us come to terms with our own past and be liberated from its tyranny. We need to know, in particular:

First, why the gods came. Why did human beings everywhere come to see themselves as being surrounded by an invisible realm of supernatural influences, spirits, and gods? And what is or was the *point* of this belief? It seems wrong simply to dismiss it as nothing more than mere error or superstition. (As Wittgenstein once remarked in another context: "For a mistake, that's too big.") We need a better account than has been given so far of what the gods taught us, and why we could learn it in no other way.

Second, we need a new theory of the twilight of the gods. If it was (as I shall argue) from the gods that we originally got all our ideas about a coherent settled order of things, a cosmos, a domain, sovereignty, law, property in land, values, selfhood, destiny, and more besides, how and why did the gods eventually work themselves out of a job and begin to slip away from us?

Setting out to answer these questions, I put forward a new linguistic theory of religious practice and religious objects. Very briefly, it runs as follows:

1: As both philosophy and religion have in the past taught, there is indeed an unseen intelligible world, or spirit world, about us and within us.

2: The invisible world is the world of words and other symbols.

3: The entire supernatural world of religion is a mythical representation of the world of language.

4: Through the practice of its religion, a society represents to itself, and confirms, the varied ways in which its language builds its world.

The idea is that, if I can persuade you to accept this inter-pretation of the religion of the past, you will not be *quite* so indignant about my proposal for the religion of the future.

As so often before, I owe a debt of gratitude to various friends and colleagues for their criticisms and their help. Among them, I should mention in particular Hugh Rayment-Pickard, Linda Allen, and, at Basic Books, John Donatich and Linda Carbone.

Cambridge, England
December 1996

PART I

THE COMING
OF THE GODS

ONE

Souls, Spirits, and Gods

The language in which supernatural belief is expressed has become slack in the past few generations—so much so that it seems that the distinctions between a soul and a spirit, and between a spirit and a god, are being lost. Until modern times, fairly clear and agreed-upon standard conceptions of soul, spirit, and God prevailed around most of the world. For the sake of the discussion to follow, I need to recall them.

Soul (Hebrew: *nephesh*; Greek: *psyche*; Latin: *anima*) is the principle of biological life, sentience, and movement. An animal body that is animated or ensouled lives and moves; but without its soul it is dead meat. The soul is usually associated with the blood (blood = life = soul)—as a slain man's blood drained away into the ground, so his soul was thought also to be going down into the Underworld. There it lived an unhappy and shadowy half-life, because, it was believed, disembodied souls feel very weak and naked. Indeed, according to Aristotle, there is some doubt about whether a discarnate soul can still maintain a person's identity. Certainly in the

3

works of St. Paul and other ancient writers, the souls of the dead yearn to be "reclothed," or resurrected in new bodies.

In this view the soul is simply part of nature and sounds as if it is merely a leftover, a rather objectifying and prescientific way of explaining what biological life is. But in a number of traditions we also find at work a tendency to supernaturalize the soul and declare it immortal, like a spirit. Insofar as the human soul is rational, Plato may see it as being most at home in his noumenal world of timeless intelligible Forms, and Aristotle may see it as participating in universal and cosmic Objective Reason. Similarly in the religious tradition, a human soul that draws close to God may come to participate in God's own nature as immortal spirit. This idea is found in the New Testament (II Peter 1:4), and the British anthropologist E. E. Evans-Pritchard (1956, pp. 60 ff.) describes something very similar arising quite independently among the Nuer of the Sudan, in their concept of *colwic*.

Spirit (Hebrew: *ruach*; Greek: *pneuma*; Latin: *spiritus*) is very different from soul in that it is not normally embodied. Rather, it is active, free-ranging supernatural power, often winged and almost always exceedingly busy, delivering messages, causing trouble, helping, chivying, and tormenting. Notice here an obvious big difference between a god and a spirit: whereas a god typically sits enthroned, over the cosmos on a mountaintop or in a temple where he receives worship and hands out the law, a spirit is seldom portrayed seated, and never legislates. It is too *busy*, coming and going like the wind with which it is often compared. And it is not usually worshiped. On the contrary, many spirits are not even known by name, but are mere anonymous members of swarming "hosts" such as the heavenly host and the Legions of Hell (see, for example, Serres 1995).

By contrast, notice that just about every god has a name, and names matter a lot. That is because gods are so territorial. They are landlords, rulers who are determined to ensure that their peoples, within their territories, know and respect their holy names. The gods employ great numbers of spirits to be their courtiers and run their errands for them. But spirits do not as a rule employ other spirits in that way.

Spirits, or powers (Greek: *dunameis*), may be objectified as individual beings in very varied degrees. Sometimes they are pictured as being no more than hands or *ankh* symbols at the ends of sun rays: they are subpersonal divine *energies* in ancient Egypt and in late Byzantine theology, scarcely at all distinct in their activity from God himself. Something similar is true of Grace, *mana*, Wisdom, the Tao, and the divine Names, all of which are only semipersonified as distinct beings. Angels (= messengers) and demons are a little more individuated—but you will find on reflection that you can name only five angels at most, and scarcely any devils at all. Lists of four, or sometimes seven, great archangels are given in the ancient Jewish literature; but we remember an angel's name only if we remember a story in which he does a particular job. As for demons, they do not seem to have stable identities.

Spirits enter into five main types of relationship with humans. One metaphor, that of pouring or infusion, suggests that spirit is like a liquid that God pours into people until they are *filled* with the spirit. Otherwise, a spirit may be your *guardian*, or may *inspire* you, *indwell* you, or *possess* you.

Some spirits seem to exist mainly, or even solely, as characters in sacred stories. They are sometimes called mythic beings, archetypal figures who have performed archetypal deeds. To draw close to such a being one must identify with him, or assume his or her persona in a ritual dramatization of the myth; and thereby one can be guided through a major crisis or transition in one's life.

By supplying us in this way with archetypal or standard patterns to follow, many spirits are rather like picturesque versions of the platonic Forms. Thus the Muses "personify" the various arts, tutelary spirits also "personify" the places and nations they protect, totems "personify" the various animal and plant kinds, monumental maidens "personify" the Virtues, demons "personify" various diseases, other spirits fill and activate cosmic zones such as the sky and the earth, and so on. As Claude Lévi-Strauss showed in relation to totems, when we consider together the whole range of spirits that a people believes in, we see it has an important epistemological function. It classifies the environment: it structures the world. The whole system teaches us to recognize different natural kinds and features of the world via personalities or personifications that not only are memorable but also prescribe appropriate responses and behaviors. In short, the spirits are very like the place names on a map of hill country: they make the world more interesting and negotiable.

We turn next to the question, What is a *god*, and how do gods differ from spirits? This distinction is not as clear as the soul/spirit distinction, chiefly for historical reasons.

Ancient Egypt illustrates the problem very neatly. In Neolithic times, as agriculture spread, many different peoples, tribes, and clans were attracted to the fertile valley and delta of the river Nile. They came, they settled, and they brought their gods with them. In those very early times, a "god" was the sort of being who might variously be described as a mascot, a tribal fetish, a clan divinity, a symbol of the solidarity of the group, or a totemic ancestor in animal form, somewhat like today's Russian Bear or New Zealand Kiwi.

During the predynastic period a unified Egyptian state and religious system gradually evolved out of this zoo of human clans and their animal patrons. They gradually became assimilated to each other. Like their human followers, the divinities gave up wandering and settled down. Indeed, they took on a more nearly human appearance as they came to reside in stone temples, where they received daily services from their priests. Gradually the whole country became politically unified under the Pharaohs, and theologically unified (more or less) under the presidency of Ra the sun god, who was also the personal god and the symbolic father of the Pharaoh.

This complex history explains why foreign intellectuals from Herodotus to Freud have felt able to say such varied things about Egyptian religion: that the Egyptians worship animals, that the Egyptians have 700 gods, and that it was nevertheless the Egyptians who taught monotheism to the Jews via that character with the suspiciously Egyptian-sounding name, Moses. The same history helps to explain how the term *god* came to signify such an uncomfortably wide range of beings, and also why theologians remain stuck with too wide a range, because for historical and traditional reasons they must claim that the ancient—and, it seems, originally theriomorphic—clan divinity, the Bull of Jacob (Genesis 49:24), is one and the same Being as the God of St. Thomas Aquinas and the God of modern believers. (In order to conceal the embarrassing truth, there is a convention that the phrase "Bull of Jacob" is to be translated as "Mighty One of Jacob": see your own English version of the Old Testament.)

Our tradition is so ancient, and has evolved such a long way from its origins, that the very word *god* has become vague. It has acquired too wide a range of uses. So for the purposes of the present discussion, I am proposing to tighten up the definition of *god* considerably. This involves a return to the core use of the word, which was pretty well understood in antiquity.

In this core use, a god was above all a *lord*. He was not a free-ranging nature spirit, always on the move, but a rather humanlike figure who sat enthroned in a stone temple at the heart of the ancient city. He was surrounded by a court of ministers and was the focus of an elaborate daily and annual routine of worship, the calendar of feasts being linked with the agricultural year. He was a vividly individual personal presence with a name that had to be hallowed, and he was a speaker who revealed his will and laid down the law. The territory over which his writ ran, and the people to whom he was covenanted, together made up his domain. His role, indeed, was to bind the holy people to the holy land and to their annual round of agricultural tasks. He was even the first great landowner and *rentier*. He was the first tax collector because tithes, dues paid in kind to the Temple, were kept in its storerooms and granaries, perhaps originally because it was essential that next year's seed corn be kept sacred, and because in any case the agricultural surplus was needed in order to maintain the cult.

In the view that I am putting forward, the old mythologies are correct in reporting that the gods were the first kings, the first landlords, and the first upper class. It is reasonable to postulate that belief in gods of this core type developed slowly in the period after 7500 B.C., when farming and fixed settlements began. The gods embodied, and indeed they just *were*, the massive concentrations of sacred authority and disciplinary power that were needed in order to evolve the first state societies. Quite simply, the only way you could make a nomad into a citizen was by putting the fear of a god into him.

The philosopher Thomas Hobbes correctly recognized that there is something ultimate and unsurpassable about the state when he described it as Leviathan, a "mortal god." The god was what it took to create the first state societies and all the new institutions they would require, which is why theistic religion is so often *established* religion. The throne of the god was the center around which the state was focused. Divine authority was the source of all later forms of public authority, the sacred realm was the first public space, and divine service the first form of public service.

The ancient connection between the sacred realm and the public realm held until the Enlightenment; but then it began to be argued by the first theorists of liberal democracy that the two realms ought to be separated. They won the argument—but they have bequeathed to us a world in which, increasingly, religion is privatized, the state marketized, and God problematic.

＝TWO

Why Spirits?

Belief in spirits is found in all, or almost all, human societies. It takes various forms, but typically a spirit seems to be an invisible, quasi-human agent that is immediately, and almost instinctively, postulated as being the cause of a sudden, strange, and unexpected event. We are particularly prone to start talking about spirits if the event has a direct bearing on human good or ill fortune. We say wryly that we must have pleased or offended "someone up there."

Interestingly, even people who usually think we can keep our thoughts to ourselves nevertheless take it for granted that our minds are wide open to spirits. These beings can descend upon us at any time, and there is no way to keep them out. Indeed, almost any bodily or psychic convulsion may be attributed to the action of a spirit. "Bless you!" we say when someone sneezes. Spirits are thought to invade our psychology, to inspect and mingle with our thoughts, and to manipulate us in any way they please, unless they are countered by the action of some greater and more powerful spirit agency.

Witch doctors, magicians, and exorcists are religious professionals who are believed able in this way to call upon one power to cast out another.

Notice in this connection that spirits are rather like male animals at the time of the rut: they love to contest with each other, to determine which of them is the strongest.

But why should anyone hold any of these beliefs? Why are people so strongly attracted to beliefs that are so perplexing and questionable?

A very popular answer was classically stated by Edward B. Tylor (1871), and has been restated more recently by Robin Horton (1970) and Stewart Elliott Guthrie (1993). It runs like this: because we are such highly social creatures, we are very strongly predisposed first to seek personal explanations of events. In daily life we have the habit of scanning our social environment very closely, picking up small signs and clues, and framing hypotheses (often, *narrative* hypotheses) about other people's doings, and their thoughts and feelings toward us. We need to know what's going on, where we are, what to look out for, and where we stand in the eyes of others. Not many of us are scientifically trained, but nearly all of us have very sensitive antennae for detecting the nuances of other people's feelings toward us. And given the importance and the profitability of using these antennae in our social environment, it is not a bit surprising that we should try using them also to interpret goings-on in the natural environment, and even within our own psychology, as signs of the activity or the attitudes toward us of unseen quasi-personal beings.

Hence religion. For Tylor, religion is just animism. Horton stresses the structural similarities between the way traditional thought explains odd goings-on in terms of the action of spirits and the way scientific thought seeks to explain the same events in terms of the operation of impersonal laws. His point is that animism is not intellectually arbitrary; it is, after all, a quest for explanation. Once we have a good narrative *explanation*, we will have a good chance of being able to take appropriate *action*. And Guthrie similarly, while insisting that all religious thought is anthropomorphic, also stresses that it is not wholly illogical. For example, a man who on the basis of a few ambiguous cues decides that "they" are out to get him and takes precautions accordingly may never actually be proved to be mistaken, and may just possibly be right. A touch of overinterpretation, whether one errs on the side of optimism or on the side of pessimism, may well be a sound perceptual strategy. As they say: "Better safe than sorry."

Furthermore, most human beings believe that what they call "life" itself ought to have—must have—a Meaning; and by a *Meaning* they mean an overall narrative explanation in personal and purposive (or teleological) terms. And people reckon themselves to be entirely capable of knowing and fully entitled to know what it's all about. So strongly do they think that there is a big Answer, and that they are entitled to expect it to be made known to them, that any news whatever, good or bad, about what's really going on behind the scenes is highly interesting and welcome to them. Isn't that why we all have such an insatiable appetite for inside stories, revelations, and conspiracy theories? And if it is true that people's deepest intellectual desire is for this thing called Meaning, then it follows that people in general are dyed-in-the-wool animists. They are convinced that there just has to be a Meaning-of-it-all, and therefore Someone to whom it all means something, Someone who himself means something by it all, and gives us various legible clues.

So, for Guthrie, religion is pure anthropomorphism; and because religious belief systems set out to meet the strongest of all our cognitive demands, and because they meet them in a way that is not wholly irrational, it is not at all surprising that there is in all ages a lot of religion about. Tylor at this point adds (his Vol. 1, pp. 133ff.) a deservedly famous discussion of how it comes about that systems of belief in which there is almost no truth can easily survive almost indefinitely.

Tylor's explanations apply very well to the case of astrology, which still flourishes three or four centuries after it was finally exploded by the rise of scientific astronomy. But the case of astrology also suggests a counterargument. For astrology does indeed resemble a religion, but the occult forces whose operation it posits are not personal. As is also true in the case of many other modern alternative belief systems and therapies, and in the case of nontheistic religions such as Jainism and Buddhism, it does seem possible for there to be a system that delivers at least something of the Meaning that people are looking for without being anthropomorphic.

There is a further argument: even if a good deal of modern belief in spirits is anthropomorphic, that does not seem to be how the belief in spirits first began. Modern angels may be anthropomorphic and cuddly, but the cherubim were once fearsome winged lions, and seraphs were winged serpents. In the remotest antiquity people probably did believe in spirits; but their belief was probably *not* anthropomorphic, because ideas about human personality and human psychology were as yet very undeveloped. On the contrary, the first collection of characters with a wide range of varied and vividly distinct personalities were not humans but the gods— for example, the gods of ancient Egypt. And where did the gods get their vividly distinct personalities from? Not from *us*, but from the animals they had formerly been! The comical, paradoxical fact is that animals had distinct characters before we ourselves did—and thereby hangs a tale.

The first fully modern humans appeared about fifty thousand years ago. They were hunters, and they produced art from the beginning. And the evidence of their art, as everyone knows, suggests that for obvious practical reasons they observed the differences between different *kinds of animals* much more closely than the differences between different *human individuals*. Indeed, clearly individuated human faces are almost unknown in art before the Iron Age, with the solitary exception of certain royal persons in XVIII Dynasty Egypt, such as Queen Tiy and perhaps Nefertiti—but we must not anticipate. The vital point is not only that we looked very closely at animals long before we learned to look closely at ourselves, but, still more, that *the universal is much older than the singular*, as the kind is older than the individual. What the Paleolithic artist drew on the cave wall was not a portrait of any particular ibex, boar, or bison but the species—the ibex, the boar, the bison. Like us, the artist saw the individual beast not as an individual but as one of a kind. It was the kind, or class, whose normal appearance and behavior must be studied closely. When you went out on the hunt, it was the image of the kind that you had to hold in the forefront of your mind until it guided you to an individual specimen of the kind, your prey. The kind preceded the individual member of the kind, and the kind will continue forever, long after you have slain and eaten the particular individual you are currently stalking. Individuals come and go, but the kind endures.

Steven Mithen (in Renfrew and Zubrow 1994) has argued interestingly that Paleolithic intelligence was (or, rather, was at first) much more domain-specific than is usual among us. Mental life in the Stone Age, he says, was "modular," meaning that although people had developed considerable skills in certain areas—social interaction, tool making, and natural history being the chief ones—these domains were at first rather distinct. There was no particular biological pressure to synthesize them. But Mithen suggests that with the transition to the Upper Paleolithic, people did begin to synthesize their various cognitive skills in such a way (it seems to be implied) as to form for the first time a more unified mental life, selfhood, and world view.

Against this background one can glimpse the function of early belief in the totem, the clan divinity, and the animal spirit. Before the rise of philosophy it was not easy to grasp what the *kind* or the universal term is, what the common noun or class name stands for, and how it unites the many in one. To this day we still use various badges of membership—

often with an animal or plant kind as the symbol on the badge—in order to make our common membership of a group vivid to ourselves. The badge or mascot is a sign of the universal. We still introduce the word *spirit* to give a little extra charge to our talk about moral qualities, abstract ideas, and so forth, as when we talk of a forgiving spirit, team spirit, the spirit of Christmas, and so on. And along similar lines, one can readily see how it would help the hunters to reify the kinds that they hunted, in spirits or totems that they could, as it were, hold before their eyes as they searched. Thus the reindeer spirit is itself the great and exemplary Reindeer, the ancestor of all individual reindeer, which controls all reindeer movements and may guide the hunters to find them. In short, the reindeer spirit is a picturesque way of thinking the *concept* "reindeer," the class term, the common noun.

In his classic discussion of this topic, Claude Lévi-Strauss quotes the philosopher Henri Bergson: "man treats an animal, or even vegetable, species, and sometimes an inanimate object, with a deference that is not entirely dissimilar to religion." Why? "To recognize a man means to distinguish him from other men; but to recognize an animal is normally to decide what species it belongs to. . . . An animal lacks concreteness and individuality, it appears essentially as a quality, and thus essentially as a class" (Lévi-Strauss 1973, pp. 166ff.). Bergson writes as if he thinks that it somehow comes easily to us to perceive the class first. It does not: the situation was that the prehistoric hunter-gatherers could survive only if they extracted enough food from the environment, and they could succeed in finding wild game or edible plant food only by paying very close attention to the species—its appearance, its habit, where it could be found, its annual cycle, and so on.

So it was a harsh, driving biological necessity that created the reindeer spirit as a *bonne à penser*, a device for keeping everyone's attention concentrated upon the kind rather than the individual. Thousands of generations of this discipline left us with a conviction that the universal is somehow logically prior to and more real and permanent than the particular, a conviction that Plato built into Western philosophy and that has lasted right up to modern times. Even today, it remains a typical mark of conservative thinking to deplore individualism.

In Paleolithic art the search for the essence of the class comes out most clearly in the way the artist seeks to capture and crystallize the distinctive way an animal *moves*. And this intense concentration upon the differences between classes was eventually to have an impact upon the rise of psychology. For, as noted earlier, when along the Nile valley a great variety of clans and tribes came together to form the Egyptian state, they pooled their various theriomorphic clan divinities. The human cultural world grew very much bigger and more complex, with both people and gods living in permanent houses. Not surprisingly, the gods then acquired human bodies. But they kept, for many purposes, their old animal heads and more than a little of their old animal natures—which is why, to this day, we still see people's characters in terms of animal models. People are hawkish, sheepish, bovine, or vulpine; they are snakes, jackals, or pussycats. A Malaysian people, the Ma'Betisék, acknowledge the complex two-way relationship between humans and animals in a most interesting fashion. In different parts of their belief system, they maintain *both* that we are descended from animals *and* that animals are descended from us (Karim 1981).

With the passing of the centuries we have tended to forget how prominent animals once were in religious thought. But in Exodus 32 Aaron makes a bull-calf of gold, and the people are portrayed as ready to believe that it is an image of the God who brought them from Egypt. And, as we saw earlier, in Genesis 49:24 God is actually described as the Bull of Jacob (in the Hebrew).

Furthermore, in the course of the history of thought, the archaic world of spirits was transformed by Plato into his Intelligible World of general ideas or Forms. Later again,

Plato's world-above was transformed by Kant into an order of concepts in our minds, and that in turn was transformed in modern philosophy (in the 1930s) into the vocabulary of our language. Telescoping the whole of this long and complex process, we now see from our point of view that the magical supernatural world of religion was, all along, a mythical representation of the world of language.

Thus, demythologized spirits turn out to be general words, and the huge power of the spirit world over the world of sense experience turns out to be the huge power of language to form, order, and classify reality. Words are the demons that can so easily slip straight from the external world into your inmost thoughts and trouble you so deeply, and words are the winged messengers that you send out to accomplish your varied purposes. Words are invisible public objects, hovering about me now as I write, in their multitudes, like swarming spirits. Language is the supernatural power that has called us out of nature.

The thesis that the supernatural world of religion is a metaphorical—and, indeed, a mythical—representation of the world of language may seem strange. Yet the analogy between words and spirits is extremely close.

In the Hebrew Bible—and no doubt elsewhere, too—a "word" may be an individual word, a sentence, a message, or a single complete speech act, such as a prophecy, a threat, a blessing, a curse, a promise, or a commandment. God's words are thought of as active powers. They remind us of spirits via their relation to God's breath:

> By the word of the Lord the heavens were made,
> and all their host by the breath of his mouth.
>
> Psalms 33:6 (RSV)

God's word travels around tirelessly like a heat-seeking missile, until it finds its target:

For as the rain and the snow come down from
   heaven,
and return not thither but water the earth,
making it bring forth and sprout,
giving seed to the sower and bread to the eater,
so shall my word be that goes forth from my
   mouth;
it shall not return to me empty,
but it shall accomplish that which I purpose,
and prosper in the thing for which I sent it.

Isaiah 55:10ff. (RSV)

In the Hebrew Bible, then, a word—and especially a word
of prophecy declaring the divine will—already seems to be
something very like a spirit agent, a messenger, angel, or
minister.

In Christian thought God's eternal Word does actually
become a person, a human living in time. Begotten in God's
heart from all eternity, he is sent forth into the world, to live
and die among human beings. The Word of God Incarnate
then gets turned back into words, the Word of God Written
(*Verbum dei incarnatum, Verbum dei scriptum*); and in Christian ritual the gospel book has traditionally been treated as if
it were Christ. So a message became an eternal Spirit, who
became a human being, who became a text, which in turn is
symbolically a person again.

Notice too that just as all human beings inhabit worlds
that are thoroughly ordered and formed by human language,
so Christ, being himself the Word of God, is in theology pictured archetypally as God's agent in creation. He is the
model world-building word.

Words are very like spirits in being invisible public objects, strangely ubiquitous. If you are yourself a writer or a
wordy person, surely you think of words as *swarming*, hovering in susurrating multitudes just like spirits. Typically they
seem to be at the forefront of one's mind, on the tip of one's

tongue, somewhere on the interface between subjectivity and the public world.

Like spirits, words are to a considerable extent self-moving: they speak us at least as much as we speak them. Swarming, they rustle or whisper in our heads; but when a cluster of them becomes closely bonded together, their collective voice becomes louder until they form what is almost a subpersonality. This object is what Jung called a *complex*, and what others may still prefer to describe as an *inner demon*.

To get power over our evil spirits/inner demons/complexes/obsessive thoughts, we must use stronger words to break them up, defeat them, bind them. Above all, we must *name* them. While they are still an anonymous legion that we can't see clearly, they are very fearsome. But when they have been named or interpreted by the analyst, they lose their power. They are demythologized.

I mean this brief account to indicate, first, why I have argued that the entire supernatural world of religion is a mythical representation of the creative—and also demonic—powers of language; and, second, why the turn to language in late modern and postmodern philosophy is having such a great impact upon religious thought.

☰THREE

The First Gods

I have proposed a tightening up of the use of the word *god*, which yields a simple working model: I see belief in spirits as typical of the old nomadic order, and belief in gods properly so-called as emerging with the rise of the first state societies. For there to be a state, there had to be a stable and acknowledged center and source of legitimation and power—and that the god supplied. The god's immortality guaranteed the continuity of the state.

The Paleolithic and nomadic human being wanders over the world without feeling any strong impulse to transform it. He has developed a good collection of the skills necessary for survival: social skills, minute observation of the ways of animal and plant kinds, weapon and tool making, and the hunt. But his thinking is rather modular, and therefore his selfhood and his world picture are rather loose-knit and plural. He believes in spirits that are wanderers like himself, and his mythic world is full of conflicts and transformations, like himself. His religious attention is held chiefly by the enduring and self-renewing kinds that he detects behind the surface phenomena of the world.

The Neolithic and settled sort of human being is surprisingly different. He (using the masculine pronoun again, but only for convenience) labors to transform a stretch of the natural environment so that it comes to express an ideal cosmological vision—and that means a world that is ordered, harmonious, law-governed, and familiar. Neolithic man is relatively much more disciplined than his predecessor—and therewith also more of a disciplinarian. He trains and prunes things. He begins to domesticate animals from about 8000 B.C. in the Zagros Mountains of northern Iran, and plants, mainly wheat and barley, from 7500 B.C. in Anatolia and, later, in Mesopotamia. Permanent villages, in the form of honeycomb clusters of one-room huts, begin to develop, and in them a wide range of craft skills are cultivated. Towns and then cities follow, each city having as its principal building a temple dedicated to its patron god. Streets first came into being, it seems, as processional ways leading with suitable dignity toward the detached houses occupied by the gods.

The god may previously have been a tribal totem or clan divinity in animal form or a fertility figure like Inanna and Dumuzi, but now he or she begins to look much more like a monumental human being and increasingly tends to become an enthroned absolute monarch. The god is seen as having unified and set in order not only the city-state but also the cosmos. (In this connection, it is vital to grasp that *the state itself is the first great cosmological model*, the first example of a fully controlled and ordered world.) Now the god becomes the focus of a daily—and annual—routine of courtly service, the cult, which is maintained by a large college of priests. They manage the god's affairs in his name and on his behalf, collecting his dues and rents, administering his domain, and interpreting his will. As part of the agricultural surplus supports the city and the temple complex, so the priests in their turn further expend a part of it in animal sacrifice to the glory of the god.

Against this background, human beings now have a much more unified cosmology and form of selfhood. Everything is unified around the god, who has set everything in its place and has established all the routines.

The god operates at two levels. While receiving his daily worship in the temple on earth, he is simultaneously holding court upstairs at the cosmic level. He sits enthroned atop the sacred mountain, or above the glassy firmament of the sky, where his ministers are a heavenly host of stars, angels, and lesser divinities. Whereas spirits are a mobile and rather unpredictable lot, a god's throne is established forever and his cult is established forever. He is immortal, a fixture. He will not change. Suppose that a plumb line were dropped from his heavenly throne down to his earthly seat. That line would run down the *axis mundi*, the axle of the world around which everything turns; and the bottom of the line would rest on the Primal Mound, the little hump of earth emerging from the primeval waters, upon which the god had sat when he first created the world and set everything in its appointed place. And to the present day the god still sits in just the same spot, radiating out his forming and organizing sacred power in all directions. He was, he is, the first monarch, absolute sovereign, and landlord.

In Israel, when the possibility of having a human king was first mooted, God was offended, seeing him as a potential rival. The Egyptian way of avoiding conflict between palace and temple was for the pharaoh to unite in his own person the roles of king and god on earth. He forestalled potential opposition by having swallowed its likeliest source. But in Sumer it appears to have taken a little time for human, "secular" kingship to develop alongside the hierarchy (a word that, by the way, means government by a college of priests). The first kinglike figures were called *lugul*, "big man." Later, the kings were seen as lineal descendants of the gods. The king, as a sort of godfather to the gods, gave the temple military protection, and in return the temple validated his rule.

This whole grand system was established at Uruk by about 3800 B.C. The Hebrew Bible (or Christian Old Testament) gives in its opening eleven books, from Genesis to I Kings, a familiar account of how Israel's version of the system became established and, in the psalter, some magnificent documents of its worship. The whole ideology has existed around the world in a great range of forms and began to decay only after A.D. 1500. Even yet something of it lingers in Islam, in the person of the Dalai Lama and the kings of Thailand, and in the coronation rites of England and Japan.

So religion-based throne-and-altar agricultural civilization dominated the world for about five or six millennia. Yet there is something very paradoxical about its central theological idea.

In the first place, the core of the whole system is the placing of an infinitely great point-concentration of sacred power and authority at the center of the city-state. This is an extraordinarily grand and awesome idea. It is an absolute idea. But how can one even begin to imagine such an idea as having evolved historically? How can one imagine some clever person first thinking it up and then somehow persuading others to adopt it?

And yet at the same time, and telling in quite the opposite direction, the great Bronze Age vision, while hugely magnifying the divine, then places it not in nature but at the heart and center of the purely manmade realm of culture.

Here we should pause a moment to consider the word *culture*. In Latin the verb *colo, colere, colui, cultum* means "to till the ground, to tend and care for." In antiquity it had already gathered the wide range of extended senses it still has today. Culture is the familiarized, tamed, gardened version of the world, which we establish around ourselves. Cicero calls it a "second Nature." It includes not only the *cultivation* of the soil, *agriculture*, but also the *culture* of new varieties of domesticated plant, the careful *cultivation* of acquaintanceships and skills, of one's own "person" and one's own soul, and therefore also *high culture*, the arts and sciences, and above all the *cult*, the care and tending of the gods. So the very word *culture*, by the way its many uses fan out, shows something that many people have understood perfectly well since antiquity, namely, that the whole range of cultural activities in a high civilization is produced by a series of symbolic transformations of the activity of the poor ploughman tilling the soil. (Especially after he learned how to irrigate and how to harness a pair of cattle to the plow, in about 4500 B.C.)

So then, if we compare the hunter-gatherer and his spirits with the citizen-farmer and his god, we notice a sharp paradox. Spirits wander freely in the wilderness: they are not at all human, and know nothing of the law. By contrast, the god is far greater than the spirits. There is something ultimately terrifying about the idea of a god. *But he's a townie!* Iconographically, he's little more than an outsize human, locked into the state establishment that his power holds together. He is purely cultural, almost immobilized in his house in the city center. He is a kind of prisoner, as all kings are.

In a certain sense the paradox has always been admitted. For it was human beings themselves who built the city, constructed the temple, carved the image of the god, established the cult—and then promptly declared that on the contrary, it was the god himself who had chosen the site for the city, handed down the design for the temple, instituted the sacrificial system, and appointed the priesthood. Thus religious ideology tacitly admits the paradox by going to great lengths in its efforts to conceal it. People were quite determined to hide the fact that they had made it all, by declaring in retrospect that the god had revealed it all.

There is more: for if we now ask, "When did the whole grand system first appear, and how has it developed?" we get an odd answer. On present knowledge, as mentioned earlier, it seems that the system appears fully formed and complete in about 3500 B.C. (I give that date because by then a simple pictographic script was becoming available, enabling the priests—already *clerici*, clergy, clerks—to be the god's really efficient accountants.) But of how this remarkably powerful system evolved, our knowledge is rather sketchy. Can one say more than that it developed because it was necessary? It is such an all-or-nothing, absolutist ideology that one is not sure how to begin to think of its history.

This last remark raises the question, "How can we study the archaeology of religion, anyway?" Six millennia of agricultural civilization have left us obliged to work on the assumption that religion is a distinct but especially important sphere of life. So the archaeologist looks out for a palatial building near the center of the settlement. It may contain special artifacts, implements, vestments. There will be, perhaps, a major audience-hall and subsidiary offices occupied by a small army of religious professionals. A library, storerooms, a treasury. At Uruk we do indeed find something like this, all roughly homologous with what might be found at a medieval Christian site 5,000 years later. But earlier, at Jericho and the great Neolithic villages of Çatal Hüyük and Hacilar in Turkey (c. 7000–5500 B.C.), we do not find the classical setup, and we realize that we don't quite know how to interpret the scraps that we do find. This in turn shows how partial and unsatisfactory our concept of religion is: we are able to recognize with confidence as being "religious" only the developed type of religious system that we already know. We don't have the concepts that would (for example) enable us to identify and describe a state of affairs in which religion truly exists but has not yet become a distinct, central, and uniquely authoritative sphere of life.

But there is a still more difficult question. What exactly was the god, anyway? Was he an emperor with no body, just a fiction, a communal illusion conjured up by a hugely grand charade? The mime Marcel Marceau can persuade his audience that his way is blocked by a huge sheet of plate glass. We can't see the glass, but Marceau somehow makes us believe it is there. Is that how the cult persuaded the people of the reality of the god? There need be no question of trickery. Perhaps in Neolithic times people in general were subject to very great needs and pressures that drove them, entirely sincerely, to postulate the god and to worship him in the way they did; and perhaps each individual believed in the belief of the group as a whole—just as armies obey orders and go into battle because each individual, even though privately he is scared witless and knows that war is madness, somehow finds himself being swept along by and believing in the solidarity and courage of the army as a whole.

Yes: but what then *was* the god? It is a mistake to suppose that the god was something over and above the image of wood or stone that was venerated in worship. You could point to the image and say, "*That* is the god," without error, because the god was a sign. He was his own image, and there was no superior referent. Each and every Donald Duck image published by the Disney Studios really *is* Donald Duck himself; there is no superior original. Donald Duck is a vivid character to millions, maybe billions, but he simply doesn't need to have any existence outside his own iconography. It would be a pedantic mistake to try to establish the existence of a real Donald Duck independent of the standard image, and then to investigate whether the standard Donald Duck image is in fact an accurate likeness. No, the vitality and cultural influence of Donald Duck does not depend at all on any such question. It depends entirely on the vitality of his image and the way it behaves. And because signs are infinitely multipliable, and each of them is the real thing, Donald Duck can be omnipresent. So it is with the god. His image *was* his reality. He was not a being but just a sign, and as the case of cartoon characters and figures such as Uncle Sam and Santa Claus shows, it is perfectly possible and indeed very easy for someone who is only a sign to be a vivid and influential personality known to everybody. Every culture has dozens, perhaps hundreds, of such figures.

So the wooden or stone image *was* the god, just as the plaster image *is* the Virgin Mary; and grown men put on curious vestments and slaughtered oxen before an image, which was the god, who was a sign—but what of?

Today virtually all human beings are citizens of state societies, and we find it difficult to grasp imaginatively the sheer magnitude of the transition from the life of a nomadic hunter-gatherer, a wild man, to the life of a citizen-farmer. But when the hunter-gatherers stopped, built huts, and established fields, they were committing themselves long-term to the establishment not only of institutions such as property and a law code but also of a fearsome and superhuman center, to which they would pay dues and from which in return they would receive protection.

Against this background one may see the god as being something like the spirit of the state; he or she was a sign of its unconditional and even cosmic authority, its searching disciplinary demands, and the security and prosperity that it promised. A good example of the way early city-state religion symbolized, and helped to teach, a new way of life is its emphasis upon the clock and the annual calendar. Nomads hate being kept to strict timetables, but state religion emphasized their importance. Millennia before the invention of clocks, it was already insistent upon the disciplinary value to the individual of keeping to regular daily hours of prayer, while the peasants in the fields found their annual round of tasks very closely mirrored and dramatized in the liturgical year. To this day the Vatican still has an Observatory and publishes a calendar: the old annual cycle of agriculture-based festivals is still maintained, and in some places the Angelus rings out yet across the fields. So for six millennia or more, religion functioned to turn wanderers into settled farmers, binding the people to the land and to the annual cycle of the seasons.

FOUR

The Coming of God

What is God, and how did modern-type belief in God first come into being?

I am not—not for the present, at least—talking about monotheism, which is a doctrine in metaphysics and which, if it has ever been coherently stated (which I doubt), began very late. What I am talking about is religious theocentrism.

The question of whether one or more gods do or do not exist is quite different from the question of religious theocentrism. There are many philosophies, such as Epicureanism, and religions, such as Jainism and Buddhism, in which it is said that though the gods do exist, they are not concerned about us and we should not concern ourselves about them. The gods are irrelevant to religion, which in the Buddhist tradition typically concerns itself not with prayer to a god but with meditation and with calmness and clarity of mind.

So, by belief in God I mean a religious outlook in which God is very important, and indeed central to life. But whether or not any gods actually *exist*, that is a distinct question. Indeed, I am proposing to show in due course both that we should now give up the idea that God "exists" and that we should nevertheless believe in God (or, at least, come to see that the idea of God is still of use in helping us to become ourselves and to live well).

So what is belief in God? The capital *G* is a clue, because it turns "god" into something more like a proper name. You can't invoke god. You'd have to invoke Isis or Athena. But you *can* invoke *God*. So when we write God with a capital *G*, it is as if the entire divine and supernatural realm has come to a new focus, which is being invoked, called upon in a personal way. We are not talking about congregational worship, nor about the invocation of an individual named god of the old sort, but about what is often called "personal religion," religion of a new, individual, and questioning type. As we shall see, the emergence of "God" in about 1750 B.C. or so coincides with, and indeed is the very same thing as, the emergence of a more individuated human selfhood standing in a new relation to the world.

In his fine study of Mesopotamian religion, Thorkild Jacobsen (1976) distinguishes a series of stages in its development. He begins with the earliest period for which we can hope to have any clear evidence, the *fourth millennium B.C.*, at a time when the cult of the shepherd-god and fertility figure Dumuzi was very popular in Uruk. Here, as in many similar cults in the ancient world, the myths and songs of wooing and wedding, death and lamentation, appeal strongly to our feelings and bind the great events of the human life cycle into the annual cycle of the seasons in nature.

However, this type of religion is still rather Paleolithic and archaic. Rejoicing and lamenting, the worshiper seeks ritual identification with the universal forces that are discerned at work in nature. One merges oneself into the god—meaning that, in sex and in mourning, we lose our separateness and pass over into the universal. Good and consoling stuff, indeed—but it does not do full justice to the new reality of political life in the city-state. The ancient temple, remember, was also a market, because it was a place of exchange where dues were collected and goods were traded. Religious thought needed further to develop the idea of a deal or contract between the gods and humans. So in the *third millennium* we find the gods becoming more humanized and political. They are rulers; indeed, they are the very first kings. The cosmos itself is seen as a polity, an extension of the state and in the image of the state—so much so that phrases like "the animal kingdom" continued in use until very recent years. With the growth of population in Mesopotamia, there is more military rivalry among city-states, so the city is now fortified; the temple complex in particular looks like a great stronghold. We now hear more about a covenant or bargain between the gods and their people. The bargain is a unilateral gift of the gods to men: the established setup in which you find yourselves is divine and perfect. It will protect you, provided that you for your part pay your dues and are loyal to the god even unto death.

The very same bargain remains the basis of our social life to this day. In the early nineteenth century, the state could still seem optional because millions of human beings were not yet citizens of state societies, and Karl Marx could even envisage the withering away of the state; but today virtually all human beings are glad enough to enjoy the security of a state society, a legal system, and a cash economy. Everywhere it is taken for granted that the state may, when it must, conscript the young men into its army and require them to give their lives in its service. Interestingly, we have scarcely yet thought out whether one day young women may be conscripted and sent to mass slaughter along with the men, and on just the same terms as the men, in some future rerun of World War I. Perhaps we do not care to remind ourselves of just how savage and brutal the demands of the god and of the State have traditionally been.

When things get as bad as that, however, has the god fully kept his side of the bargain? Early in *the second millennium* in Mesopotamia and elsewhere, we find that military defeat and political instability are forcing people to question the fundamental contract on which civilization has always rested. We were originally told, remember, that the gods established a perfect—and surely disaster-proof—system. They knew what they were doing: they knew everything and could see everywhere. Just look at their huge eyes! They are all-powerful. We were assured that if we played our part, kept the law, paid our tithes, and maintained the state cult, the gods for their part would guarantee peace and prosperity. So what went wrong?

A similar question arose at the level of the individual life, as people began to become conscious of individual human beings and their very varied fates in life. The overall political-theological setup is universal, and the same for everyone. So why does one person seem to be graced, the favorite of the gods, glowing and charismatic, destined for great things, while another suffers one disaster after another?

The peculiar difficulty is that the official state theology talked entirely at the universal level. Only the universal counts: that was the old philosophy. But in the second millennium B.C., and for the first time in human experience, it was being realized that there is another level, that of the individual, and at the individual level it too often looks as if human life is ruled by pure amoral and unpredictable contingency—in which case public assurances handed out by the great and the good at the universal level are utterly worthless to us. In every civilization from the Bronze Age to the present day, the common people have been gamblers, believers in fortune who know that life is a lottery—and we should not be surprised. That, indeed, is how it looks to them.

The difference between the sexes makes the question here still more poignant, because although women have always lived more in the universal than men, their personal fates in life are even *more* and not less arbitrary. Women's lives have always been more dominated than men's by the great universal experiences of the reproductive cycle: love, marriage, sex, pregnancy, childbirth, child rearing, aging. But their relatively deeper involvement with these universals seems only too often to make women's happiness more precarious rather than more secure. For tens of thousands of years, we have been taught to seek consolation in the universal. The contradiction is that woman is both more universal than man and yet also even more vulnerable to pure contingency.

At the time in the second millennium when people first began to worry about individual happiness, and individual fortune and misfortune, something like modern belief in God began. In Bronze Age times the gods represented and personified the entire divinely ordered scheme of things, the fixed political and cosmic establishment within which human life was lived. Religion was originally just a way of identifying yourself with it and *into* it, ritually. Then (in the third millennium, as I have suggested) religion became a way of committing yourself to the setup politically. You paid homage to the god as your king. But now at last religion offered a vocabulary in which the individual could emerge and question the entire arrangement. At that moment the gods become God, because then the whole divine order was called to account by the individual, and in the form of a person. And at that moment, one may say, Israel emerged as the one who doesn't just worship God and obey God but who strives with God. Abraham (Genesis 18:22–33) has the religious courage to take on even Yahweh himself, and he prevails. That is faith—to beat God down.

What is new about belief in God, beginning around that time, is that it brings into sharp conflict the individual and the universal. It courageously and impudently makes human selfhood cosmic. The afflicted individual presumes personally to take on the entire cosmic scheme of things—as if it were all no bigger than he is. (He's right: it *isn't!*) Out of that desperate presumption the self and God are born together.

The questions that can be put to God are varied. They open up the whole future of selfhood and religious thought. In particular, one may ask either, "Why have You done this to me?" or, "What must I have done, that You should treat me like this?" To see the difference between those two questions is to see why the personal relation between the believer and God was the biggest, most dramatic, and most complex personal relationship dealt with in late Bronze Age writing. As we see in the Hebrew Bible, which continues all the same themes, the dispute with God becomes the classic arena in which selfhood is elaborated and human subjectivity is produced. Nowhere else do we find such psychological riches. The psalmist moves from ecstatic adoration to bitter reproaches to penitent submission and then to joy and gratitude. Prayer was the classic method of investigating and exercising the self, opening speculative thought and stretching the soul, and the relation to God thus developed became a resource utilized in the construction of many other human relationships, such as courtly love in the Christian Middle Ages.

At the end of his life, Michel Foucault became interested in "technologies of the self," or the means by which selfhood is produced and cared for. He noted the importance of "spiritual exercises" and techniques of the self in early Christianity, but he took a rather negative view of their effects:

> Christianity requires another form of truth obligation different from faith. Each person has the duty to know who he is, that is, to try to know what is happening inside him, to acknowledge faults, to recognize temptations, to locate desires, and everyone is obliged to disclose these things either to God or to others in the community, and hence to bear public or private witness against oneself. [Foucault 1988, p. 40]

In Foucault's view Christianity was interested in stretching, enlarging, developing human subjectivity only in order to make more complete the self's ultimate subjection to divine power and the authority of the Church. It is sexier to have a slave who really *knows* that he is your slave.

That, however, is a little too narrow a verdict, which must be modified if we go farther back and see how, ever since the beginning, challenging God and striving against God have been constitutive of belief in God. In the parable of the Unjust Judge (Luke 18:1–5), Jesus commends the importunate widow not for her resignation and docility but for her ceaseless nagging and complaining. In the Hebrew Bible—and not least in the Psalter, which is read through over and over in the Western service books—the relation to God always includes the element of *chutzpah*, argumentative impudence and pertinacity. And Foucault might have gone all the way back to Egypt and Mesopotamia to find the forerunners of Job (for example, Pritchard 1969, pp. 589–91). Belief in God began when an individual first had the cosmic cheek to call upon the system to justify itself. Crazily, he said: "I call You to account," and that call made the gods God.

Thus modern-type belief in God began not with somebody thinking up an argument for the existence of a god but with the *questioning* of the gods and the beginning of critical thinking. It is very striking that among the Jews, Abraham is remembered not only as the founding father and a great hero of faith but also as a trickster and as someone who does not hesitate to dispute with God. And that old Jewish impulse to complain to God and to question God has survived into modern times and can be illustrated from the Jewish response to the Holocaust, whereas the Christian church has been so obsessed with increasing its power over its own membership that it has almost always insisted upon repressing doubt and dissent. As a result, the God of Christians has become oddly blurred and remote.

God, then, I am suggesting, began with the possibility of questioning God. God and human subjectivity were born more or less together, and God has ever since functioned as the mirror in which we look to become ourselves.

There is a small piece of confirmatory archaeological evidence. In ancient Egypt the pharaoh Amenhotep IV (or Akhenaten) is famous for having invented an idiosyncratic version of monotheism, and in his age were produced the earliest-known vividly individual portraits in the history of art. An ebony head of Akhenaten's mother, Tiy, is the best single example. She really looks like an old queen who is somewhat worried about her difficult, eccentric son (and she was not, you may think, the last queen to find herself in such a position).

Now, if it is the case that belief in God, with a capital *G*, arose at a time of emergent human self-consciousness—when the human individual sought to define himself vis-à-vis the whole scheme of things, by standing back from it, even personifying it, and then arguing with it—then we can see the possibility of a new interpretation of what it means to believe in God. God is here being thought of as an imaginary personification of the whole scheme of things, and therefore as one who is to be loved, praised, thanked, grumbled about, argued with, and questioned. And we may go on to think of God as a spiritual ideal, a reference point, an ideal, and a focus of aspiration.

Along such lines, we may be able to develop an account of religious faith in God that is independent of philosophical monotheism. We would learn to separate the poetical and religious use of the idea of God from the philosophical doctrine that there does in fact exist an infinite and eternal super Being, who transcends the world and is the ultimate ground of all existence and all value.

Can we in fact separate the God of religion from the god of the philosophers? Most people seem to think not. We live at a time when the god of the philosophers, the really existing, all-powerful Being out there, is rapidly fading away, and people are tending to assume that when he dies, religion dies too. That is a pity: we can do better than that.

FIVE

God and Greek Philosophy

Two widely different accounts of the place of God in Western culture have jostled against each other during the twentieth century.

One of them, most popular around 1850–1950, saw *ethical monotheism*—philosophical belief in an objectively existing God—as a central intellectual pillar of what used to be called Western Civilization. This latter phrase was most often employed in connection with Europe's "civilizing mission"—its duty to spread its own culture around the globe. What had given to Western culture this special destiny? It saw itself as having arisen from the confluence of three very different streams: the Jewish ethical and religious genius, Greek philosophy, and the Roman gift for law and large-scale organization (not to mention imperial conquest). In the formation of Western culture the meeting of biblical faith and Greek philosophy had been critical. From it had issued the Christ-

35

ian *philosophical theism* that gave Europeans their peculiar crusading energy. They believed in one God and in one great world historical narrative. In their colonial, missionary, and commercial outreach to the rest of the world, the Europeans could see themselves as co-workers with God in the working out of his good purposes for the whole human race.

At the opposite extreme, a dissenting tradition derived from Nietzsche and Freud dismisses *realistic* or philosophical belief in God as worthless, and instead says that God should be seen as an imaginary person, a literary personality who has become a popular myth and still occupies a unique place in the imaginations of about half the human race. The other half consists mainly of the peoples of South and East Asia, who are simply not familiar with either philosophical monotheism or the stormy God of the Hebrew Bible.

This God, the Yahweh of the J writer in the Hebrew Bible, is described by Harold Bloom (1991) as being like a powerful and uncanny male child, a sublime mischief maker, impish and difficult. He resembles Lear and the Freudian Superego in being a demonic and persecuting father, entirely lacking in self-knowledge and very reluctant ever to learn anything. Like J's other characters, he has a continually changing consciousness. He manifests the pure energy and force of Becoming. He is Nietzschean will-to-power, abrupt and uncontrollable, subject to nothing and nobody.

These are two amazingly different *placings* of the idea of God, so different that they vividly illustrate the extreme disorder into which our religious thought has lately fallen. One God is an expression of world historical optimism; the other is something like an archetypal image of unreconstructed maleness in the human psyche. But on the whole, the turbulent century just ending has witnessed a gradual shift from the former picture of God to the latter. In Britain, W. G. de Burgh (1923) still believes that there is such a thing as Christian civilization, built around a Judaeo-platonic philosophy of God, the world, the soul, and history. But C. B. Cochrane (1943) and R. G.

Collingwood (1940) give more than a hint of strain; and, from a German-American point of view, Paul Tillich (1951) and H. R. Niebuhr (1952) explain why. It now appears that the young Tillich was already in 1919 a Nietzschean, who saw himself as a Christian theologian writing after the death of God, and who knew that old-style culture-Christianity had come to an end with World War I (Tillich 1987).

So in the 1950s belief in ethical monotheism as the basis of a coherent Christian civilization was finally coming to an end, and death-of-God writing began to become more explicit even within Christian theology itself. An early consequence of the shift was indeed a readiness to look in a new way at the psychological history of the God idea in the human imagination (Jung 1954). And perhaps we are now ready to take a further step. Perhaps it is time to cast a cold eye at Greek philosophy and how it gradually became interwoven with Jewish and Christian faith to produce the realistic philosophy of God that our churches are still, anachronistically, stuck with. Was it all a misunderstanding? During the twentieth century we gradually became accustomed to the idea that historic "orthodox" Christianity got Jesus of Nazareth very badly wrong. Are we next going to have to recognize that it made a somewhat similar mistake about God?

Martin Heidegger (1889–1976) has already put forward an interpretation of the history of Western thought along these lines, arguing that from Parmenides and Plato onward, the gradual objectification of Being as an infinite, all-powerful Person-out-there, the God of Western realistic theism, was an intellectual—and a religious—disaster (Heidegger 1987). He's right, of course, and indeed the way the Church got God wrong was closely related to and tied up with the way it got Christ wrong. (In both cases, something light and dialectical was turned into something heavy and lumpish.)

Our discussion so far has suggested a number of new theses about the rise of philosophy and its cultural-religious consequences.

In the first place, Greek philosophy did not come from nowhere, and there is not such a sharp break between philosophical and prephilosophical thinking as some writers have suggested. For example, we saw that, in order to succeed in getting food, the Paleolithic hunter-gatherers were forced to become expert in recognizing stable natural kinds, natural forces, and calendrical regularities as underlying the flux of experience; and they had to recognize a sense in which the universal precedes the particular and even produces it. When you went out hunting, you had to have that universal at the forefront of your mind and on the tip of your tongue, until you encountered something that answered to it. So it helped you to find your prey.

The Paleolithic hunter called this thing that guided him a spirit, Plato calls it a Form, Kant a concept, and I call it just a word. But formally, or logically, the guide and the procedure are much the same in all these cases.

Plato and other Greek philosophers also continue Bronze Age thought in their readiness to slip back and forth among different levels: psychology, politics, cosmology; the self, the city, and the cosmos. The philosophers are, nearly all of them, apologists for law and order. They want things to run like clockwork, law-abiding, benign, and harmonious at all levels: so that Plato will readily argue that just as in a well-governed state everything *would* be done in obedience to wise and benevolent laws, so at the cosmic level that is surely how everything actually *does* happen—and therefore, of course, *ought to* happen in the state and, uh, in our own souls too. He argues from a conditional *ought* here below, to an actual *is* above; and thence back down to substantive *oughts* here below again. Because we want law and order on earth, we know it must already exist in the heavens and *therefore* must also be brought into effect down here on earth.

This is not only entertainingly illogical but also highly revealing. Plato comes closest to theism in his most political works. In the *Timaeus*, in particular, he develops the idea of a divine intelligence that forms and rules the world, ordering everything for the best. You can trust the Great One who is in charge. He knows best. Such is Plato's doctrine of a divine providence, which has had a big influence on Christian thought; but in retrospect there is everything wrong with it. It is a piece of political ideology; it jumbles together two utterly different meanings of *law*, the civil and the physical; it works only at the level of the universal and simply disregards the caprice of our individual fates in life; and it is empirically and scientifically plain wrong.

Thus in different ways the new philosophical sort of thinking was by no means as detached and innovative as it pretended to be. Older constraints, whether biological or political, were often still operative.

Second—and a related point: much of the vocabulary of philosophy is in fact the old vocabulary of religion, somewhat demythologized or diagrammatized. For example, the old word for *Fate* (*Anangke*), when suitably laundered, becomes the new word for *necessity*, logical and also metaphysical. Even the word *theory* (*theoria*, a view or spectacle) itself has a strongly religious background, so that theory was originally not a disinterested and purely cerebral look, but on the contrary a participatory, religious kind of gaze that did you good, like seeing God or seeing the Elevation of the Host in Christianity (Urmson 1990).

In sum, philosophy arose not as an entirely new way of thinking but rather by the secularization of much older—and often religious—patterns of thought.

Third, Greek philosophy was from the first—and certainly was in Parmenides and Plato—very strongly "realistic" in orientation. Whereas Buddhist philosophy sought freedom from suffering and calmness of soul, Western philosophy was oriented mainly toward knowledge of the Real. Objective knowledge was priced high, with top standards of certainty, evidence, and lucidity; and the Real, in the sense of something other than ourselves and overwhelmingly bigger than ourselves, was something very powerful, beyond time and change. (See Rorty 1991, especially pp. 27–49.)

Why does certain and objective knowledge of the Real thus understood make us *happy*, and do us good? The suggestion is always that we will somehow come to share its attributes—its immortality, its perfection, its goodness—and so will be able to escape from our old, bad, timebound selves.

Such is the claim: and my present conclusion is simply that realistic theism—in the sense of belief that there really and literally does exist an infinite and super-Real all-powerful Person out there to whom we must above all else get closer—owes most of its strength to the way the Greeks originally set up the project of Western thought. The biblical writers are happily far too diverse, poetic, and wayward to be seen as having any single view on the matter. And I shall argue (in chapters 9 and 10) that the way Jesus of Nazareth used the word *God* was emphatically Jewish and not Greek—questioning, not philosophical.

SIX

Where Are the Gods?

The philosopher Ernst Cassirer once wrote:

> Man has, as it were, discovered a new method of adapting himself to his environment. Between the receptor system and the effector system, which are to be found in all animal species, we find in man a third link which we may describe as the *symbolic system*. This new acquisition transforms the whole of human life. As compared with the other animals man lives not merely in a broader reality: he lives, so to speak, in a new *dimension* of reality. [Cassirer 1944, p. 24]

I agree with Cassirer that human beings were originally driven by their biological needs to evolve the rich and complex world of symbolic meanings within which all our life is now lived. What he says, however, does require at least one important qualification. It no longer seems quite accurate to define *man* as the *animal symbolicum*, in view of the huge growth of knowledge about animal symbolic communication that has taken place since Cassirer wrote. The social and communicative life of animals turns out to be far richer than used to be thought.

Is it still important to try to pick out something that is distinctively and uniquely human? If so, then it cannot be just symbolic communication, or tool using, or a complex social life, or perhaps even art: it will have to be found in something that develops rather late, namely, human subjectivity. The main stages in this are:

1. Human cognitive abilities cease to be merely modular, and are instead synthesized to produce a more unified consciousness and world-view.

2. The flow of symbolic expression gets to be complex enough to turn back upon itself and to comment upon itself, thus making *self*-consciousness possible.

3. As, in early Bronze Age times, the gods get to be both more powerful and more human, the relation to the god gets to be more complex and dialectical. It becomes a school of subjectivity, human selfhood being elaborated and developed in and through the relation to the god.

4. Finally, in early monotheism, "God" is postulated as a fictioned antagonist, a personification of the whole scheme of things, who is questioned, praised, reproached, argued with; and now the self and its Other are *co-equal* disputants, language runs unstoppably, and the human project is fully launched.

According to this account, God did create us—at least in the sense that we became ourselves by first postulating and then slowly gaining the courage to argue with our gods. And Nietzsche was right to describe the Hebrew Bible as the best book in the world, because it is the book of the one religion that above all others is *not* just a system of worship but something far greater—an argument with itself. In the view I am proposing, biblical theism is always toppling on the edge of, and often falls into, atheism.

A question may still be asked about the symbolic order: Why did it have to take this curious form, and what is its status? I mean, just what are the gods, and where is their abode? What are we nowadays to make of the whole strange supernatural world of religion? A good deal of the history of thought could be written as the history of our various answers to these questions—or perhaps I should say our various *transformations of* these questions.

Some worthwhile hints are given within religious language itself. *In the first place*, the supernatural world is always pictured as being elsewhere and not here. It may be set in a mythic past, in the far future, in the world above, at the top of the sacred mountain, or at the bottom of the sea, or even in a Pure Land over the seas: but it is not here. There is evidently a very clear intention to signal that the world of the gods is not the everyday world.

Yet, *in the second place*, it is also insisted upon that every single moment and spatial point in the everyday world is exposed to the view and the action of the sacred world. Each event and each object in the everyday world has an archetype in the heavenly world, or is brought about from the heavenly world. Thus in theism, although God lives in heaven and is unseen, he is also omnipresent on earth, where he controls all events.

The two worlds are, then, both clearly distinguished and deeply interwoven. And *in the third place*, it seems to be assumed that every human being is as it were preprogrammed to recognize the distinction between them. You may read bedtime stories to children for ten years—stories about witches and giants, magic and talking animals, stories with a most elaborate supernatural apparatus—but never once will you hear your children complain about the implausibility of the stories. They accept them without demur, and understand exactly how to take the stories, where to file them away, and what future use to make of them.

Just what is it that our children understand so well but that we have forgotten? In a word, children recognize from certain little cues that are usually given at the beginning of a story that the supernatural world is transcendental. Not transcendent, but transcendent*al;* not above, but presupposed; not data, but programming; not given *in* the world of everyday experience, but supplying the standards and patterns that are to be applied *to* the data of experience. Supernatural stories do not give information; they program the mind.

But this is to anticipate. For the present, we simply keep in mind the three clues: the supernatural world is other than the everyday world; it nevertheless touches the everyday world at every point and supplies all the patterns in terms of which the everyday world is constructed; and somehow every child knows what it is and how it works.

What, then, is the history of the supernatural world, the world of humanity's ideal culture? I have sketched it through a series of stages. Already in Paleolithic times human beings, in order to survive, had to pick out and to concentrate their attention upon a range of enduring plant and animal kinds and natural regularities that underlie the flux of experience. People had to distinguish between the fleeting individual and the relatively enduring universal kind or pattern of which it is a specimen; and they had to recognize the priority of the kind. This they did by representing the universal as a totemic ancestor or a spirit, which was thought of as somehow controlling all the members of its kind.

It was at least as difficult for the early hunter to keep his mind on the job as it is for a modern person. He was no smarter than we. But he had to succeed in the hunt, a task that required intense care and concentration over a period of many hours. This was achieved by "personifying" the kind he was hunting, in the totem or the spirit. The hunter went out "possessed" by the image or spirit of the creature he was looking for. And that state of possession—brought about by a variety of ritual means such as dance—was the first human state of great intellectual concentration. It worked. We survived: we are here.

In its earliest form, then, the supernatural world of religion was a world of spirits that represented and controlled the various natural kinds, forces, and regularities, and the major cosmic regions. It was a symbolic representation of the natural world, of an especially authoritative and practical kind.

In Neolithic times the supernatural world of religion had to change in order to impose upon people the new and even stricter discipline of a state society. The spirit-beings now become much more powerful and authoritative—and more human too, because the world is now a much more settled and differentiated human social world. So the spirits become gods, and the gods represent human tasks like metal working and harvesting, moral qualities like wisdom and justice, and social roles like the lawgiver, the warrior, and the farmer. But the supernatural world still remains a world of universal archetypal figures and deeds that set all the standards and prescribe all the forms.

Perhaps all—or, at any rate, most—of philosophy is demythologized religion: certainly Plato, inheriting this legacy, redescribes the world of gods and spirits in the language of philosophy as a "noumenal" or intelligible world of universal, standard-setting Ideas. And to him it seems to be a really existing, mind-independent World Above. Perhaps all those people who believe in objective moral and intellectual standards agree with him still.

At a further stage in the story, during the Christian period, a curious backtracking and doubling-up takes place. The whole world of ideas finds itself getting taken up into the mind of God, where the Divine Ideas are seen as the archetypes of created things; and yet at the same time the Ideas also find themselves getting converted into *eidola* and then into *angels*, who are tutelary spirits—executants of the divine will, guardians of persons and groups, and embodiments of various natural powers and qualities (thrones, dominations, virtues, princedoms, and so forth). And there is even a third way in which the one God is connected to a plural world: through the Eastern Orthodox doctrine of the radiating divine *energies*.

Then in the philosophy of Kant, there is another reversal. The world is turned inside out, and platonic realism is converted into German Idealism. The entire world of Ideas is suddenly internalized, not now in God but in *us*. Instead of being transcendent, it comes to be seen as transcendent*al*; that is, it comes to be seen as an internal programming by means of which *we ourselves put a construction upon* our own experience. The everyday world is not Formed by an antecedently existing world of Ideas out-there: it is Formed by us, in and through our knowledge of it. The World of Ideas is no longer a really existing objective world, but has become an inner and presupposed programming of our own minds. (For example, our optic nerves clearly cannot carry three-dimensional space into the visual cortex. What happens is that we must presuppose three-dimensional space a priori, and then fit the stream of incoming visual data into it.)

So Kant transformed the old Objective Order of intelligible essences and standards into a framework of categories and concepts, around which we build our world.

Now the story starts to get really complicated; but all we need here is the last stage in the argument, in which Kant's order of transcendental categories and concepts is finally translated into, simply, *language*—and now the whole process ends by coming full circle. Paleolithic human beings already had language, and language itself already contains the common nouns and other general notions that are what this entire story has been about! The history of human thought has been the history of our discovery of what was all along implicit in our language, our first and greatest invention; and the supernatural world of religion turns out all along to have been in various ways a mythical representation of the truly magical world of linguistic meaning.

Does this seem a strange doctrine? But religion was all along obsessed with language. Everywhere people take it for granted that gods have names, that gods are language users whose utterances are words of power, that gods can be spoken to, and that all the business of religion is transacted in language: scriptures, commentaries, instruction, sermons, rites, formularies, creeds—and heresies too, because God is the master of meaning and because he demands strict control of language. Hence religion's intense concern about language, and the fear and anger that are aroused by "bad" language, blasphemy, and any slippage of linguistic meaning.

The argument goes like this: religion has always understood that our world is formed and our life is ruled by our language. That much, at least, is true. The vision of the world as a fully formed and stable divine creation, a cosmos, depends upon God's own complete mastery of linguistic meaning. To hold the world steady, we must keep all our linguistic meanings stable and unchanged, using words in just the way God used them when he first set up the entire scheme of things.

Decoding becomes easy when we recall how strong the linguistic metaphors originally were in the Christian doctrines of the Logos and of the Trinity. God is the Speaker. Christ is the Logos, his Meaning, begotten in his heart and sent forth to do his will. The Spirit is the moving, activating power of language. God's Almightiness and his unchangeability guarantee the stability of the whole world of meanings, and therefore the stability of the language-formed cosmos.

On analysis, then, we find that religious supernaturalism comes down to linguistic supernaturalism. (*Linguistic supernaturalism* is the belief that the meanings of words—or of some key words—are absolutes, immutable, fixed out-there and objective.) Now we see why the study of *divinity* was the study of "scripture" (that is, writings) or "sacred letters," and why there was so much *learning by heart* of religious texts. The divine realm simply *was* a fixed and canonical system of linguistic meanings. While they held steady, the world held firm and the old religious systems held firm. We today live after two or three centuries of freedom of speech and rapid cultural change: we may fail to remember how strict traditional society used to be about the control of meanings and forms of words, and why it all seemed to matter so much.

PART II

THE DEPARTURE
OF THE GODS

⹀SEVEN

Mysticism

Before the rise of philosophy, religious language was (I have suggested) poetical, disciplinary, and shaped by the practical and social needs it met and the uses to which it was put. It is anachronistic to ask how literally people then took their beliefs, because for the most part they didn't yet have any notion of speculative knowledge of a real extra-human order of things. For them, the question of literalism or realism did not arise, and it is sufficient to look upon their signs simply as signs.

So by seeking to remain within their horizons, we have found that *the soul* is a sign of life; that *spirits* are signs of the forces, qualities, and kinds that most need to be recognized; that *gods* are signs of power and moral authority; and finally that *God* is a master word that comprehends the whole scheme of things within which we live, personifying it in a way that we will often want to worship and sometimes to reproach.

It is worth interpolating here that the uses of the word *God* overlap with a surprising number of other words that are used to much the same effect: *fate, luck, chance, history, things, it, it all, life, the throw of the dice, destiny, time, how it goes,* and so on. We notice the similarity between these words and *God* when we begin to notice small regional differences. Thus, where we may say "It's hot today," in parts of Africa people say "God's hot today"; and where some people say "God will judge," others say "History will judge" or "Time will tell."

These considerations may suggest that there is no more to be said about the word *God* than may be gleaned by close attention to its current uses. But Greek philosophy, of course, attempted much more than that. From an early stage, it consciously sought speculative knowledge of the objectively Real, a reality that might be viewed either as an order of intelligible essences or as pure self-existent Being. In this contemplation the philosopher hoped to find eternal happiness.

Being thus oriented toward the knowledge of something supremely Real, intelligible, valuable, and blessedness-giving, Greek philosophy was clearly likely to move in the end toward some form of realistic theism. And in fact a developed religious philosophy of God slowly took shape during the first four or five centuries of the Common Era. The key names are those of the Jewish writer Philo of Alexandria, the philosophers Albinus and Plotinus, and the Christian writers Origen, the Cappadocians (Basil the Great, and the two Gregories), Augustine, and the pseudo-Dionysius. Because Augustine has fully assimilated what it means to say that God is infinite and that all things depend upon the divine will, it can be said that classical Abrahamic monotheism of the sort still maintained by many or most Muslims, Christians, and Jews was first and best stated and understood by Augustine.

Even as the doctrine of God was developing, however, acute problems that have never been solved were also surfacing. Already in Philo (for example) it is said that God is altogether transcendent; but if God does indeed transcend the categories of our understanding, then he must elude our comprehension and must be indescribable in our language. This consideration is perhaps traceable right back to Plato's *Republic*, but see what follows from it: the postmodern "crisis of representation" started with God, and started near the beginning of the Western tradition. It was in the area of *theology* that thinkers first found reason to wonder how human descriptive language can be thought of as hooking on to or encompassing its topic. And if this question of how language can be thought of as pinning down and fixing something supposedly outside and distinct from itself, once clearly asked, turns out to be unanswerable, then it appears that realistic theism was an impossible project, doomed from the outset.

Even worse problems arose when, after Plotinus, God came to be thought of as infinite and having infinite attributes. For God's infinite attributes must *nihilate* by comparison everything that is merely finite and creaturely; and when, in the tradition of Western theology founded by Augustine, every thing and every event has come to be thought of as utterly dependent upon the decree of an infinite and inscrutable sovereign will, the result is a positivism so extreme as to verge upon nihilism (Gillespie 1995). The world is reduced to disconnected bits, each of which is as it is because God willed it so, and that is that. Human beings cannot expect fully to understand anything, ever, except by a graciously granted supernatural illumination of the mind. The concern for secular knowledge is unprofitable, vanity, curiosity—in a word, *sin*. After Augustine, culture is destroyed, the only rational way of life is the monk's, and the Dark Ages are inevitable. Such was the disastrous end of the great classical tradition. How did we escape? Eventually, Arthur Kroker seems to suggest, Nietzsche reshaped Augustine's doctrine of the *divine* will to will and made of it the basis for a renewal of culture by the *human* Will to Power. This has cheered things up, because we may have some hope of understanding a world that we ourselves have willed (see Kroker and Cook 1988, pp. 58–62).

In this view it may be suggested that the doctrine of an actual infinite God is incoherent, destructive, and a cultural catastrophe. But that is too simple a view, because in justice we need to add that the very same thinkers who were developing the doctrines of God's infinite and absolute Being, will, and power were also the inventors of a deconstructive tradition. Interestingly and paradoxically, the same classical theological writer, often in the same text, may be found *both* building up a violent and nihilistic theology of absolute divine sovereignty and power *and* also subverting it by applying to it the familiar deconstructive techniques of mystical theology. Augustine is one example, but there have been many others.

The standard line of writing runs somewhat as follows: as the *archē*, the first principle or self-founding foundation of all things, God is absolutely one and simple, as well as being infinite. God has no body, parts, or passions. He has no structure. There is in God no *differentia*, no contrast, nothing that one might be able to single out or get hold of. Nor can one draw any "nearer" to God, because God is omnipresent in his whole reality everywhere, and yet also infinitely Other than us. We always already coincide with a God who is always unknowable. In contemplative prayer God therefore is apprehended only as a naked, formless void infinite that may equally well be described as dazzling light or as deep darkness, as the plenitude of being or as absolute nothingness, as fullness or as emptiness (for example, Carter 1990). And the state of resting in God may equally well be described as a state of absolute knowledge or as a state of the purest unknowing.

In this state, participating in this state, emptied out into this state, the self finds itself undergoing just the same deconstruction as God; so that just as in contemplative prayer the theism/atheism distinction vanishes, so also the self/not-self distinction vanishes. God is lost and I am lost in void bliss. Religious language becomes purely expressive and ecstatic, as in Augustine's mystical idiom.

In his later writings, it should, however, be added, Augustine presents a relatively strong human self, with a threefold structure that he seeks to use as an image or reflection of the Trinity. Thus, by looking into the mirror of his own soul, Augustine hopes to see a reflection of his God over his shoulder. God is, perhaps, his own self's Other or counterpart. In this form of mysticism the difference between copy and original is lost, however, so that Augustine once again experiences mystical deconstruction. He cannot tell whether God is a projection of his triune self, or whether his own self is a created image of the triune God. Again the difference disappears; it just doesn't matter. So prayer eventually makes Buddhists of us all, leading us into the Blissful Void.

The reason why a writer like Augustine can be found both building up and dismantling an authoritarian philosophy of God has again to do with realism. As an inheritor of the tradition of Greek philosophy, as a great churchman, and as a member of the ruling class, Augustine knows he must teach God's objective and mind-independent existence. In very troubled times it is above all necessary for the people to be convinced of the objective truth of the Church's faith, its disciplinary authority, and the terrifying sanctions in its armory. The people must be taught realism. But religion is not only a tool of social control; it is also a way of salvation. Like any other believer, Augustine wishes himself to be united with the God in whom he truly believes. And now he faces the difficulty that his realism has alienated him from God. Realism may be necessary for the common people, but it is dreadful for oneself. God's reality has been established, over against the mind, by setting up a whole series of metaphysical contrasts—between the finite and the infinite, the temporal and the eternal, the sensual and the purely spiritual, and so on. Built out of all these disjunctions, God is set up against the self like an infinite wall of smooth black marble, blocking out everything. There is no way of making any religious progress except by deconstructing all the binary contrasts by means of which the realist doctrine of God was first established.

The special literary techniques of mystical writing therefore aim to deconstruct the classic metaphysical contrasts and bring realism to an end, with an effect that is as if God and the self have been melted together. The result is usually described as a dissolving of the soul, with an extraordinary effect of religious liberation and happiness, a kind of intellectual orgasm, described by some people as "union with God" or the "spiritual marriage," but which others describe as "atheism" and wish to see punished.

The best mystical "postrealists"—figures such as Spinoza among the Jews, al-Hallaj among the Muslims, and Eckhart among the Christians—have accordingly been punished by their co-religionists. Punished for being right, because mysticism gives the game away. It dismantles God for God's sake (see Evans 1993, p. 59; Cupitt 1980; and Kelly 1977) because it must. For reasons that have to do with politics and power, the religious authorities and people at large are committed to the realistic notion of God, and no doubt will continue to be so. But the few who truly wish to attain religious happiness will also continue to discover that the way to it is by dismantling, dissolving away the realistic doctrines of both God and the self, so that the two can be melted together. Admittedly the spiritual marriage is a deadly heresy; but it is also eternal happiness.

The last irony of religion: in the end everything we most deeply longed for coincides with, and turns out to be the same as, everything we most feared. All the great distinctions and oppositions out of which we built our ideas of God, the world, and the self are undone, and the result is . . . nihilism? Bliss? Both, of course. The dissolution of God, and our attainment of perfect union with God, are one and the same thing.

⋲EIGHT

The End of
Dogmatic Metaphysics

By the later fourth century, as I have said, the Western tradition had become committed to realistic philosophical theism.

It needs to be said at once that the marriage of faith with philosophy was never entirely problem-free and happy. On the contrary, the difficulties that were eventually to bring down philosophical monotheism were recognized by some from the outset. If God is a simple, infinite, necessary Being, he must fill everything. Where is there "room" for anything else to exist that is distinct from or independent of God? How can God so defined be related to the manifold contingencies of a changing, temporal, created world? How can God be thought of as *personal*, or be described in our language? And if God is so infinitely and overwhelmingly our one great end in life, our be all and end all, must he not annihilate all other cultural concerns?

Considering these and similar questions, and considering

57

also how completely we have become committed to a thoroughly postmetaphysical view of life, we may well wonder how the old metaphysical sort of belief in God ever got to seem as compelling and as clear as it did.

The answer is that philosophical belief in God did not stand alone. It was surrounded by, embedded in, and sustained and given intelligibility by a whole raft of deep assumptions, most of which came ultimately from Plato. These assumptions were the so-called "absolute presuppositions" (R. G. Collingwood's phrase) of the old Western culture. We just didn't know how many and deep they were; but gradually, between Descartes and Derrida, they were brought to light by the new critical kind of philosophy. Once they were exposed, the question arose of whether they could be proved. Kant tried to show that they could be proved, some of them at least, but only in a way that involved giving up the old metaphysics of God. Instead of being objective truths propping up an objective God, Kant made them into just structural presuppositions and postulates of our knowledge and our moral action. Others, however, though they admire Kant's great attempt to find a compromise, judge rather that the old platonic assumptions collapsed and crumbled to dust as soon as they were exposed to the light. As soon as we could see them, we could see that they are groundless.

But what *were* the assumptions? Occasionally we hear something said that gives us a glimpse of their continuing influence. We should seize such a moment and analyze what we hear.

For example, when some years ago the senior Fellow in my college died, his successor as senior leaned toward me across the table and said in a strange harsh voice, a little grim, sardonic, triumphant, emphatic, fearful, and even envious: "Well, he *knows now*, doesn't he?"

Those words are a window. I thought about them for a few days, analyzing them backward, and came up with this:

Life

1. Truth is not manufactured by us; it is discovered by us, or dis-covers (the Latin *vela*, "veil," gives us the word *re-veals* or *un-veils*) itself to us.

2. The answers to all properly framed questions, both questions of fact and questions of value, preexist out there, objectively.

3. There is a great and final Answer to the mystery of our existence, out there, awaiting us.

4. All these truths and answers (2, 3) are, so to say, *tailored to* our faculties and our requirements. They are in principle accessible and intelligible to us, so that we may reasonably hope and expect to discover them, or have them reveal themselves to us.

5. There is then something quite *dazzling*, namely, a preestablished harmony between thought and being, language and reality; between the questions we want to ask and the Answer that the nature of things is waiting to give us. (Notice that this most astonishing doctrine is also the one most profoundly taken for granted.)

6. The final Answer will be revealed to us in or through death.

7. Our life is a pilgrimage toward death, the moment of truth, the moment of absolute knowledge.

8. Our life is a journey, then, from
   (a) the relative to the absolute; from
   (b) time to eternity; from
   (c) the changing, sensuous world of becoming to the realm of pure timeless intelligible Being; from
   (d) the particular to the universal; and from
   (e) the mediated, discursive, through-a-glass-darkly sort of knowledge, to pure face-to-face unmistakable vision.

9. Each person's life is a story scripted beforehand, and there is a great Story of Everything whose plot has been revealed to us in a Book.

That is in outline the world view, the story about the meaning of life, that my old friend was invoking at the lunch table. But this was the early 1980s, and he knew as well as anyone that every bit of it is questionable. He drew the grim, sardonic tone of his voice from the thought that death can still be relied upon anyway to settle the matter for each one of us in our turn. (He is now dead himself, so the matter is settled for him.)

That is by the way, for the moment. In #8 I introduced a number of binary contrasts. They came up while we were thinking about the difference between the way things are on life's journey and the way we hope they'll be when we get to life's destination. They are contrasts between two worlds, the earthly and the heavenly:

The Binary Contrasts

10. The binary contrasts (in #8, a–e), and a number of other related contrasts, are all analogously asymmetrical.
11. In each of the cases cited, the second of the pair:
    (a) is prior;
    (b) is superior (that is, greater in both value and reality, and therefore standard-setting); and
    (c) in some way governs or produces or brings about the first.
12. Thus the spiritual world above is in every way better and greater than this material world below.

Being and Value

13. There are degrees of reality, and of value.
14. The scale of degrees of being is also a scale of degrees of value, or goodness, or perfection.
15. The Most Real is therefore the Most Good, and vice versa: for the Highest Good is—has to be—the Supreme Reality.

16. To gain the highest knowledge, we must purify our souls and perfect ourselves; and one should, in particular, prepare for death.

We should add here a few of the principal causal maxims:

Causality

17. *Ex nihilo nihil fit* ("Out of nothing, nothing comes to be").
18. Every change has a cause; or, every thing that is has a cause of its being.
19. The cause is prior to the effect; the cause is *responsible* for, or *accounts for*, the effect.
20. The cause is superior in reality to the effect.
21. The qualities that are found in the effect preexist in a higher degree in the cause.

So the cause-effect relationship is modeled on the father-son relationship, as that was perceived in a traditional agricultural and patriarchal society. Every effect is a chip off the old block, and every created thing is a finite refracted image of its cosmic creator-Father.

For our present purposes we don't need to go into more detail here, but one final proposition is worth adding. Eastern thought is often therapeutic. It says that we are made unhappy by the violence of our own disorderly passions. When we have slowed down and our passions have become still, we may find complete happiness in a state of cool emptiness: *sunyata sunyata*. By contrast, in Western thought the supreme good is a *cognitive* state, and a state of fullness rather than emptiness. We are absorbed in contemplation of, or are swallowed up into, an infinite and eternal perfection and fullness of Being.

22. Our last end is the absolute knowledge of what is greatest, most real, and most perfect; a knowledge in which we shall enjoy eternal happiness.

Now we see why Nietzsche describes Catholicism as "platonism for the masses" and why, at an even later date, A. N. Whitehead could describe the whole history of Western thought as "footnotes to Plato": because so long as the deep assumptions (or most of them) remained in place, philosophical belief in God seemed perfectly natural and intelligible. And conversely, as in the work of the major critical philosophers (Descartes, Hume, Kant, Nietzsche, Heidegger, and Derrida), the old assumptions of Western, or "platonic," metaphysics have been brought to light and have crumbled away, so the credibility and even the very intelligibility of God have steadily faded away.

As we leave Plato behind and the culture becomes "post-Philosophical" (Rorty 1982, pp. xxxvii ff.), God evaporates. The God of realistic philosophical theism, the metaphysical God, the super-Being out there, was made possible by Plato, and dies with him. But the process is not quite complete. There are still a few philosophical platonists, and in everyday conversation we may still hear people making the contrast between the material world and a distinct spiritual dimension. It remains possible (as Kant, Wittgenstein, and Derrida all suspect) that Plato's ghost will never be finally exorcised, and people will always be tempted by the illusions of metaphysics. In which case the battle between nonrealists and realists over God will never end.

History and Humanism

You probably remember your first day at school. I can still see myself, just five years old with pale yellow hair, standing in the main hall of a Victorian primary school in Southport, Lancashire. A high roof of pitch pine with hammerbeams; a pitch pine dado running around the wall at my eye level. I look up in awe at the height of the ceiling, the number of other children, and the noise. My mother waves as she leaves. I had feared that this would happen.

The curious and significant fact about our long-term memories is that in them we see ourselves as from the outside. This is especially true of our memories of ourselves as children. By contrast, the point of view for our present experience and our short-term memories appears to be just behind our eyes and between our ears. The short-term view is individual and subjective, whereas the long-term view is that of an ideal observer in public space—the view of a novelist or film director, or indeed God's view of us.

In the short term we are subjective; in the long term we become objective. (*Objective* is Latin for "thrown out there," "fixed.") And now we begin to understand that the long-term view is the archaic perspective, and that the short-term view, the purely individual angle upon and construction of the self and the world, has been developed only since the later Middle Ages by a calculated and systematic *deferral of objectivity*.

The reason for this is that (as we saw earlier) for nearly all of human history, the objective and the universal, the God's-eye view, the public and communal construction of the world and the self, was overwhelmingly dominant. People's first sight of themselves and their world was from the universal standpoint. Objectivity really did come first, to such an extent that painters and writers had to work extremely hard at training and disciplining themselves to look upon the world simply and solely from within their own naked individual subjectivity. They had to labor to discover a personal style, an individual feel for things. Look at Petrarch, Chaucer, and the Gawain poet; look at Jan van Eyck, Roger van der Weyden, and Brunelleschi. The writer is beginning to try to tell us not how the world looks absolutely, but how the world looks to *him*, and even how the castle appears to a particular knight within the story as he rides toward it. The visual artist, similarly, is not seeking to show us things as they are in the sight of God. He is saying: "This is exactly how it has looked to *me*, from my angle, at this particular point in time." The reason van Eyck's old faces are so remarkably intense and memorable is that he really does want to teach us to see the world and one another from a finite, human, and mortal point of view. I think he'd like to convince us—as perhaps Rembrandt would also like to convince us—that the individual mortal human's perception of his mortal fellow human, in its very transience, can somehow be more real and more *detailed* than the old grand public and theological vision. Van Eyck can do both; indeed, he can sometimes show us the two visions side by side in the same work. When he paints a theological topic, van Eyck is producing a representation of a universal theme, and doing so according to canonical rules; but when he paints a patron, or some other man or woman, he is freed from the universal, free to be just one individual mortal looking at another, free to show us that the human eye is more merciful than God's.

It will be retorted that the production of subjectivity, in self-examination and in confession, is itself surely an ancient religious theme. Yes, but in that case the individual self is produced precisely *before God*, and viewed from the standpoint of eternity in a way intended only to *confirm*, and not to defer or to challenge, the priority and superior greatness of the universal. Whereas I am talking about a new form of consciousness and vision of the world that is developed, very slowly, as the outcome of a long struggle to fend off and postpone the dominance of the universal and sacred vision, and thereby to allow the fragile subjective vision enough time to come forth, establish its own distinctive character, and perhaps even prove its own superior reality.

The struggle has been very long, and the battle is not won. Religious conservatives in many faiths still detest the subjective vision, which they—understandably, from their point of view—regard as embodying a sinful and presumptuous attempt to resist and defer accepting the authority of all the ancient public and sacred norms of reality and value. Again understandably, they use boo-words like "Western individualism," "relativism" and "humanism," all of which—we should know—are very Bad.

One of the many advantages of the subjective vision, however, is that it has given us a sense of history that we are not now likely to wish to give up. While the old theological and objective vision prevailed, there could not be any very vivid sense of history, because the whole frame within which human beings live was seen as having been antecedently fixed.

You could not change the arrangement. All you could do was to keep on reenacting universals, within the arrangement and in a manner conditioned by it. In everything you did, you were recycling some standard pattern, retelling an old story. This is still true even of a writer like Shakespeare. In his day you still didn't invent an entirely new story: you retold an old one. Anything novel was sin. No radical change in the human condition could take place until God in his own good time should choose to move everything on to the next act in the cosmic drama that he had scripted and was now directing. Till then all of human life was but an allegory, each person and each act being meaningful only as an emblem of something universal. Again the universal came first, and the universal was timeless; therefore there was no real history. History comes into being only insofar as the universal is pushed back, deferred long enough to allow the merely subjective, contingent, and transient a little space to come forth in. That space, the tense of human action, is exactly and precisely what grammarians call the *imperfect*. From the longterm and objective point of view, the self and the world appear finished, and finished by God; from the subjective and short-term viewpoint, both the self and the world are incomplete, waiting to be finished by our action.

The deferral of objectivity, then, allows us to see reality as dialectical. The historical process involves an interplay or conflict of individual projects and world views, and the so-called real world is the gradually evolving consensus that results. We truly are historical agents, because through our interactions with one another we have among ourselves evolved, and are still shaping, every aspect of the "reality" within which we live. It is human historical action rather than divine creation that finishes the world.

We can use the word *interactionism* for a general philosophical doctrine, namely, the view that *everything*, including all linguistic meanings, truths, values, and indeed reality itself, is a slowly evolving consensus product, the result of an interplay of forces in the human realm. And, as I have been trying to indicate, the point of developing the short-term, individual, subjective, and relativistic point of view is that it has given us the chance to make and finish our selves and our world by our own historical action.

ᗗTEN

Culture and Language

I have been arguing that modernity began at some point in the later Middle Ages when, almost for the first time ever, a few people began to look at the world from the subjective point of view and through their own *imperfect* mortal eyes.

Hitherto the objective and universal had almost always come first. People had seen their world, and even themselves, as if from outside and through God's eyes. And because they saw the world as a cosmos, a divine creation objectively finished and complete, they could not have our sense of history. The world being already perfected, human action was limited to "doing God's will" by reenacting divinely established archetypal patterns and retelling old stories. You could recycle universal themes within the system, but you couldn't change the system.

But now the hitherto-almost-forbidden human point of view becomes established *by deferring objectivity*. This probably happened by meditation upon the human suffering of

Christ on the cross. Christ had himself experienced the with-drawal or deferral of the objective reality of God. God had against all expectation abandoned him to his own suffering and mortality, and he had cried out in despair.

Thus the merely subjective, only-human point of view had become canonized—even legitimated—within Christianity itself. It was accessible to Cistercian monks in meditation, to painters and writers. It was visible in the twisted body of the gothic crucified. Christ himself had been the first bare forked animal who had experienced our life from the human sub-ject's point of view, as pure unconsoled transience, suffering, and mortality. That is extraordinary: when you recited a Litany of the Passion, and meditated on the Passion, you were identifying yourself with Jesus in his state of being derelict, abandoned by God. Medieval monks at prayer be-gan to feel what it was like to be godforsaken. Jesus, atheous and only-human, is the first-born of many brethren, the pio-neer of modernity.

The delay or deferral of God may at first have been expe-rienced as a moment of terrible loss and despair, but (as we noticed earlier) in the later Middle Ages it quickly became extraordinarily productive. As religious art gets to be more emotionally expressive and only-human, it gets better; as people get closer to death, their faces become more interest-ing and even more beautiful to a painter like Jan van Eyck; and as thinking gets ever more skeptical and self-question-ing, philosophy is reborn.

In short, the deferral of God opens the space in which the modern world comes to birth. One after another we see ap-pearing Christian humanism, vernacular literature, Protes-tantism, the nation state, critical philosophy, science, the historical consciousness, liberal democracy, and modern technology. Christ's humanity—and above all his Passion—have allowed people in the West to see our world and our life from the only-human point of view: to see them as unfin-ished, imperfect, transient and purely contingent, and to see

truth as something we don't have and must therefore struggle to build up, testing it out for ourselves as we go along.

In Islam, by contrast, there is no moment of pure and
only-human weakness at the center of the faith. On the contrary, subjectivism and humanism are perceived as Western,
and remain firmly excluded. God doesn't get deferred: he
stays forward, filling all things, and so the objective vision
remains remarkably strong in Islam even to this day.

In the West, however, we have become committed to the
finite, and to the only-human point of view as the touch-
stone. The appeal to experimental test and to mere sense
experience, which Plato considered weak, has turned out instead to be a powerful tool for building new knowledge. The
huge growth of our science and technology now seems to
keep God firmly—or even permanently—deferred. Supernatural belief lingers because it has social prestige for historical reasons, but it is now "fringe" as far as the serious
business of life is concerned.

Even the people who profess most loudly that they hold
their supernatural beliefs in a literal or realistic sense do not
in practice behave as if they take their own beliefs seriously.
Many people claim to believe in astrology, but they do not
think of demanding from astrologers the same precisely for-
mulated and verifiable predictions that we get from as-
tronomers when, for example, they forecast an eclipse. When
a new drug turns out to have been insufficiently tested, and
either does not work or has harmful side effects, people do
not hesitate to sue the pharmaceutical company that produced it. But you never heard of a Roman Catholic success-
fully suing the pope because a visit to Lourdes had
unsatisfactory results. That supernatural belief is now everywhere just fringe belief is proved by the fact that nobody, not
even the strictest fundamentalist, seriously proposes to check
it out with the same degree of rigor we all expect in the case
of new technologies; and even in the relatively few cases
where something of the kind has been attempted, one does

not hear that any people have actually changed their beliefs as a result.

So, if we know that supernatural belief is out of date and intellectually in poor shape, why are we so reluctant to let go of it? The answer is surely that by clinging to the remains of old beliefs we can postpone dealing with the crisis that overtakes us when they are finally lost.

When human beings first began to look at themselves and their world from a viewpoint firmly inside their own finite and mortal subjectivities, they were committing themselves to history. We must *act*, to establish a shared vocabulary and shared values, to build a society, to form and finish ourselves and our world. And this implies a commitment not just to history but also to a new only-human understanding of culture and language.

In the tradition-based societies of the past, nearly every aspect of culture was thought of as having been divinely instituted, or at least hallowed by antiquity, and as being therefore unchangeable. The same was true of language. Often, words were spoken of as "names" (from the Latin, *nomina*, meaning "nouns"), the presumption being that our descriptive language names and then tracks an intelligible extralinguistic structure of the world, already built into it by the Creator. So people took a thoroughly supernaturalistic view of language. They supposed that God thinks in our language, and has formed our world by using our language. So when we describe our world we are repeating God's words after him, retracing what he has ordained. God has given us a ready-made world, and equipped us to understand its structure. Our language is divine, linguistic meanings are unchangeable, and the adequacy of language to copy the shape of things is theologically guaranteed.

The shift to the newer only-human point of view meant that eventually this entire scheme of thought would collapse. Instead, the whole of culture and language would come to be seen as embodying a historically evolving and ever-changing human consensus without any absolutes or fixed points, and without any guarantee whatever that our language hooks onto an extralinguistic-but-yet-somehow-already-language-shaped world order.

Now things start to get exciting, for now we see that we have to give up the notion that there is a stable, mind-independent world order out there waiting to be described correctly in an equally stable and adequate (from the Latin *adequatus*, meaning "commensurate, fully equal, co-responding") vocabulary. The most we can ever now hope to reach is some form of pragmatism that has given up the idea of objective truth, and is content in every department of life with ways of speaking that work well enough to get by with—for the present.

The position is that there are no absolutes or fixed intelligible essences waiting out there, able to hold at least a few of our linguistic meanings steady. On the contrary, every word in the dictionary has a history. Culture has a history. Religion, philosophy, and even logic and mathematics have histories. We do not have, and we never will have, either the standpoint or the vocabulary that would be needed to prove the truth of realism. Instead, we are caught in what some call neopragmatism, others call nihilism, and yet others describe as postmodernism. And we see that it is simply the long-term outcome of modernity (Harland 1987). The turn to the subjective and mortal human viewpoint looked enormously profitable for several centuries, but now the bills have at last come due as we belatedly realize that *of course* our world will in the end come to look as insubstantial and radically transient as we ourselves are.

Religious conservatives used to assert that one must not permit the objective reality of God to be questioned, because the death of God would inevitably be followed by the death of Man and the death of the world. They were correct, because the old philosophical doctrine of God came as part of a scheme of thought that also gave us a ready-made world to live in and faculties specially designed to know it. Nietzsche himself already clearly understood that God, the Real World, and the old notion of knowledge all stand or fall together. If they do indeed fall, then we are committed to rethinking everything. Indeed we are.

⹀ELEVEN

The Time of the Angels

The intellectual revolution I have summarily sketched has very large-scale social corollaries: the end of realism, the end of belief in absolutes, the end of belief that the world is ready-made to be our home, with all the rules to be kept already laid down and built-in. People are becoming de-traditionalized, nomadized, "casualized," as the old fixed points of reference disappear. Instead of marriage, a series of relationships; instead of a home, a series of addresses; instead of a career, freelancing; instead of a church, the irregularly mushrooming politics of protest; instead of a faith, whatever one is currently "into"; instead of stable identities, pluralism and flux; instead of society, the market and one's own circle.

These are times when the intellectual climate is very permissive, as if (outside science) the culture has suddenly become all fringe and no mainstream. Popular supernaturalism and belief in fortune, new religious movements, and New Age groups multiply exceedingly; but it's all a fad. None of it is to be taken seriously, because it is not clear that *anything* is or can be serious any more.

Many older people vehemently dislike what is happening and try to pin the blame either upon "the sixties" or upon a tiny group of French poststructuralist intellectuals. But in fact it is scarcely necessary to master Derrida's great early books in order to grasp what has happened and why, because the whole of the current upheaval is no more than the working out, accelerated by new technologies, of an idea that became very familiar during the nineteenth century: the idea that everything has a history.

People have traditionally wished to think that their linguistic meanings, their religious beliefs, their moral standards, and so forth go back to the mind of God and the beginning of the world. In Tennyson's *In Memoriam A.H.H.* (1850), we see how difficult it was even for a person of good ability to accept that, on the contrary, everything has a history, everything comes and goes. Yet every page of James A. H. Murray's *A New English Dictionary on Historical Principles* (1888) teaches the lesson that the meaning of a word is not a timeless essence, but is given by the history of the ways it has been used. What could be simpler?

Everything has a history. Linguistic meanings have histories, truth has a history, morality has a history, religious belief has a history, reason itself has a history. And of course the doctrine that everything has a history itself has a history. Result? Universal meltdown, nihilism, postmodernism. Everything indeed that Nietzsche in the 1880s was already saying so clearly; but in these matters it often takes a major thinker to see the blindingly obvious. And it is a typically postmodern paradox that the *OED*, one of the world's worthiest books, should also turn out to have been one of the most ferociously subversive.

According to Iris Murdoch (1966), the death of God is followed by the Time of the Angels. (Her novel of that title espresses her reaction to the controversies about God.) The central authority having broken down, errant spirit powers wreak havoc in the world. Nietzsche (1888, the same year as the beginning of the *OED*) is more cheerful, imagining something more like a Bacchanalian revel: with the end of realism, all free spirits run riot. But our present argument has pointed toward an interpretation slightly different again.

The world we know least about (and a world that, indeed, has come clearly into view only very recently) is the world of linguistic meaning. This world of meaning is the world that comes first; it is the real supernatural world that wraps around, that clothes, the whole of the empirical world. One might say that everything in the empirical world is *paralleled in, prefigured in,* and *formed by* this strange invisible world, the world of meaning. In short, everything that used to be said by scholars about the supernatural world of religious belief (see Bellah, in Lessa and Vogt 1972, p. 40) can be reformulated and restated as a doctrine about the world of linguistic meaning.

However, the world of linguistic meaning is numinous and fearsome. It is very often alarmingly excessive and even delirious, in ways and for reasons that Jacques Lacan and Gilles Deleuze have in their time very well stated (see Lecercle 1985). Hence it has seemed, in the past at least, that for there to be culture there needs first to be a strong disciplinary control of the world of meaning.

Against this background the main doctrine once again emerges: the historic function of the entire supernatural world of religion was to represent to us the world of linguistic meaning—a world that has always been curiously difficult to enter and to think about except through poetry and myth. Second, religion's mythicization of the world of linguistic meaning also functioned to keep meaning under control. God the first speaker was the master of meaning, its lawgiver, and the guarantor of stability.

The modern breakdown of supernatural belief is a breakdown of the old mechanisms that used to govern language and prevent it from running out of control. Hence we now live in the time of the angels, a crazy time, a time of bad language. What new sort of religious outlook might replace what we have lost?

PART III

RELIGION
AFTER THE GODS

≡TWELVE

The Legacy of the Old Religions

An extraordinary cultural upheaval is in progress at the moment around much of the world. The last few millennia are going up in smoke as millions, even billions, of people desert, forget, quietly design out or actively repudiate their ethnic, religious, and moral traditions. Some people are desperately trying to hold on to or restore their traditions but are finding to their dismay that it cannot be done: the substance of tradition is melting away, slipping through their fingers even as they try to grasp it. The loss is becoming so complete so quickly that very soon now historians will be finding it difficult to reimagine what it was once like genuinely to believe such things and follow such customs.

The reasons why it is all happening are familiar enough: rapid technological, economic, and social change; the sudden unimportance of our ancestral beliefs, customs, and values; the break with the land and the past; the rapid movement of capital, people, and ideas around the world; and the pervasive sense of groundlessness and outsidelessness. "Is that all there is? You mean, *this is it?*"

Foreseeing the present collapse of tradition, Nietzsche rejoiced. According to him, the entire "historical" period has been a lamentable digression. It has been a period dominated by negative or "reactive" feelings, by bad conscience, and by oppressive disciplinary institutions such as the State, the Church, and the Law. The typical human being has been a reduced and house-trained, or "domesticated," human. Had it not been for the triumph of *ressentiment* (Nietzsche's word for negative feelings), we might have been able to jump straight from prehistory to posthistory—from Homer to Picasso, say. Why not? For then we might have been able to cut out the ugly millennia of ill feeling, guilt, asceticism, and otherworldly religion.

So says Nietzsche. He acknowledges, of course, that the "historical" period did produce many great individuals and works of art. What of all this deserves to survive will survive. But Nietzsche has no time for the historical period's characteristic states of soul, feelings, and forms of consciousness. He seems to think that it has all been pathological and can vanish completely, unlamented.

Crucially, Nietzsche is not willing to recognize that religion has been a powerful tool of self-development by enlarging the scope of consciousness, intensifying and purifying it. He is not much interested in exploring different spiritualities and different ways of being a self and building one's world. He speaks only of forging, out of the various conflicting energies within us, a unified, free, active, and fully affirmative type of human being, the Overman or Superman.

This is a limitation, because within the old religions, now fast slipping away from us, there are (or were) a number of valuable and interesting experiments in selfhood and modes of consciousness, some of which we ought to keep.

The influence of Christianity, with its very strong emphasis on correct doctrine, may lead some people to think that perhaps one of the major faiths may be quite straightforwardly the Truth, *en bloc*. Unfortunately, that is not how things are. Scholars such as W. Cantwell Smith (1963) and G. Lindbeck (1984) have in recent decades led us to recognize that a major religion is an object that resembles a whole civilization or cultural tradition, rather than a simple and clear-cut ideological system. It is not really appropriate to think of an entire tradition as being straightforwardly just true, *en bloc*. It is not even appropriate to ask which particular religious beliefs are simply true, with a view to picking them out for preservation. It is indeed probable that several faiths preserve good historical traditions about their founders, and we can also (perhaps) describe as being straightforwardly true a very few religious doctrines that deny the truth of other religious doctrines. The main examples are the Buddhist denial that there is in us a metaphysical soul, and the Abrahamic monotheists' attack upon idolatry. But that is about all, and the conclusion must be that it is futile to look for any extant religious beliefs that can be judged to be dogmatically true and then abstracted for reuse in the future.

In brief, the position is that all our present major religious traditions are now coming to an end, just as the once very grand religions of ancient Mesopotamia, Egypt, and Greece came to an end in antiquity. As happened in the previous cases, we may expect that something of the great works of art will survive but virtually nothing of the doctrine. Most of Christian theology has already been lost, as we soon discover if we ask people to explain, for example, just how Christ's death has made atonement for our sins, or the difference between Calvinism and Arminianism, or the doctrine of the Trinity. These are—or were once—very grand and important matters, but people at large lost all knowledge of them generations ago, and it is not coming back.

What then is there in the now-vanishing religious traditions that we really want to save, and may perhaps be able to save? I am suggesting that what we should pick out as valuable and try to salvage will be certain forms of religious existence: that is, certain forms and practices of selfhood, certain modes of consciousness and ways of expressing oneself in one's life. In the future we will see our religion not as supernatural doctrine but as an experiment in selfhood.

To give an example of what I mean here, we can't save God because God has long been dead. We saw in chapter 8 that the metaphysical assumptions on the basis of which classical theistic belief was possible have disappeared permanently, and what now passes for belief in God is a very reduced version of what it once was. But the form of selfhood and the way of looking at life involved in belief in God *can* be retrieved. What in the Sea of Faith network (an informal society of religious radicals and revisionists, established in Great Britain and New Zealand) is called "nonrealist faith in God" is an attempt to salvage at least something of a God's-eye view of oneself and of our life, *after* the death of God.

Similarly, I shall argue that we can recover something of the Buddhist vision and something of an authentically religious ethic.

I thus pick out three themes that I hope we can salvage and restate in a form that might be transmissible to the future. I call them the *Eye of God*, the *Blissful Void*, and *Solar Living*. In the past, when thinking was more dogmatic and exclusivist, just one of these might have been thought the basis of a complete religious outlook on its own. But under postmodern conditions culture has become very plural, and so have people. We should learn to pursue our own personal growth by exploring and flipping among several different forms of selfhood and views of life. There is no One Great Truth anymore, and there never will be again. It is now better to maintain a small personal repertoire of different truths, paths, and goals, to be utilized ad lib.

The Eye of God

The old metaphysics of God was destroyed by Hume and Kant, and will not be revived. Many people think that to believe in God is to hold that there exists a very big and friendly unseen Superperson, but such a view of God as an outsize invisible man (or, as others say, woman) is neither clearly statable nor rationally defensible. However, belief in God can survive and can be defended if it is interpreted differently, and seen as involving a certain form of consciousness and practice of selfhood. To believe in God is to live as if under the eye of God, and to assess oneself and one's world as from the standpoint of eternity. The person who truly and seriously believes in God is a person who has a special mediated (or, as I shall call it, "bounced off") kind of consciousness, a consciousness of oneself as one appears from an ideal and universal standpoint outside oneself.

This "nonrealist" view of God has a long history. It is present when, for example, Meister Eckhart says that the eye with which we look at God is the same eye as the eye with which God looks at us. In the modern period it is most clearly and thoroughly worked out in the traditions of Kant, Kierkegaard, and Wittgenstein. It asks us to give up the old "objective" doctrine of God, and instead see talk about belief in God in terms of the way it leads us to see ourselves and shape our lives.

One sign of nonrealism in a writer is the recognition that in our relation to God there are not two distinct parties. Rather, one relates oneself to oneself through the universal. In the present argument I have been trying to show that this routing of religious thought through the universal goes all the way back to the beginning of humanity. But notice that, unlike Kant and Kierkegaard, I am not saying that belief in God is in some way obligatory. I am saying only that it is a valuable and interesting form of consciousness, worth preserving and cultivating. It is only an option—but it is a good one. We are in a new situation, in which we can say: "God is voluntary." Belief *that there is* a God is not, in the old way, necessary to salvation; but many of us continue to find belief *in* God helpful. So I say only that it is a good thing to learn to see oneself from a new angle.

Some people may still find the very idea of an indirect or "bounced-off" form of self-consciousness perplexing. But one example of it is universally familiar, and that is woman's consciousness of herself via man's view of her. Prefeminist woman, looking critically and appraisingly at her own person in the mirror, or commenting on the appearance of other women, seems to a remarkable extent to be able to look at and judge her own sex as if through the eyes of the other. Men usually have very little notion of how they are appraised by women, and profess not to know what women think or want, whereas woman appears to be justifiably confident that she knows how she appears to men and what they are thinking. As man's being around makes woman more alert and self-aware, so God's being around made the Western believer much more vigilant and self-conscious. Man's being around makes woman think about how she appears in his eyes, and God's being around made the believer wonder: "How do I appear in *his* all-seeing Eye?"

In this politically risky analogy, I have of course referred to an effect of the historical subjection of women. In Psalm 123 (Hebrew numbering) the relation between servant and master, or mistress, is used to very similar effect. Not surprisingly, humanists and feminists are critical of what I have called mediated or bounced-off self-consciousness, saying that although it may be true that being in a state of subjection can make us more subjective, it is much better to throw off subjection and try to achieve a genuinely autonomous self-consciousness—in *both* cases.

To which there are two replies. The first involves a line of argument that goes back at least to Figaro and Hegel, and probably much further. The Lord's eye, resting upon the one who is in a state of subjection, makes the subject more subjective. Being forced to consider carefully and constantly *both* how he presents himself to me *and* what my behavior looks like to him, the subject ends up with a much clearer view of *both* parties to the relationship, and therefore with better social skills. So it comes about that *of course* Jeeves is brighter than Wooster, Figaro outwits Almaviva, Woman outwits Man, and ever since Abraham the Jews have been smarter than their God.

A seriously postmodern definition of true religion: religion that makes you smarter than your god. The practice of looking at oneself and one's world as if through the eye of God—that is, from the universal and ideal standpoint—confers many advantages. It heightens consciousness, it gives one a conscience, and it helps one to see oneself and others with a greater clarity of moral vision. It also opens great humorous possibilities, which Jews and East Europeans have exploited very effectively. The God's-eye vision is also the comic vision.

And the second reply to those who think the bounced-off form of consciousness too servile for a modern person: just as even a feminist may occasionally, in order to win a tactical victory over a man or just for pleasure or for both reasons at once, revert to her old unreconstructed ways, so a Christian nonrealist like me may often find himself dropping back into the old type of God consciousness, praying or worshiping because he wants to or because it helps. And why not? I actually think I love God more now that I know God is voluntary. I still pray and love God, even though I fully acknowledge that no God actually exists. Perhaps God had to die in order to purify our love for him.

I am seriously suggesting that one can still love God after the death of God. Let me explain further.

A well-known London psychotherapist takes to an extreme the nondirective method of counseling. During sessions he sits at the opposite side of a wide table, wearing very dark glasses. His elbows rest on the table, and his head is on his hands. He sits stock-still in complete silence, the idea being to efface or depersonalize himself as much as possible. Clients are at first unnerved, and then irritated. Finally, they spill the beans. They talk and talk. Still he says nothing. They talk some more.

Hearing this, I suggested facetiously that he might perhaps reach the very peak of his profession if he were to replace himself with a cardboard cutout, or perhaps a tailor's dummy. Since he doesn't do anything, a sign of himself would be just as effective as his presence in person; and since signs are infinitely multipliable, he would be able to treat any number of clients simultaneously.

After that rather banal suggestion, a more interesting one: Would he not do better still if he were to replace himself with his own gravestone? All over the world people visit graves to talk to their dead, and as Kierkegaard says, the love we feel for our dead is the most faithful and the most purely unselfish of all our loves (1847, pt. 2, chap. 9). The dead person whom I love is infinitely silent and patient. He accompanies me wherever I go. There can be no question of deceiving him: the very idea is absurd. He is unchangeable. Fixed in eternity, he grows no older. The more Kierkegaard goes on in this vein, the more astonished one is that he fails to remark that he has given to the dead the attributes of God. Conversely, the attributes of God are very like the attributes of a dead person.

Continuing in his usual unstoppable style, Kierkegaard remarks that if you want to make someone give himself away, you must "make yourself *nobody* in conversation with him." And that is the dead person's craftiness: he *is* nobody—and therefore he has the power to draw the truth about ourselves out of us. Yet, although the dead person is nobody, we do have duties toward the dead. We tread softly and speak quietly in their presence—*presence?*—and bring little offerings of flowers to them.

The omnipresence of the dead is exactly like that of God in that although we take the thought of them along with us wherever we go, we also need a place where there is a special marker of their absent presence, or present absence. The marker—gravestone, altar, or whatever—makes us talk, and thereby acts as a midwife of truth.

Nietzsche goes on in typical nineteenth-century style about churches being the "graves of God," but it does not occur to him that we might one day visit churches in order to be prompted to talk to God, in the same way as we visit graves in order to commune with our dead, and with similar benefits.

Love for a God who is dead is a very pure—and religious—kind of love. Consider a parallel case: the purest and most religious thanksgiving that we humans are capable of is the everyday exclamation, "Thank God!" uttered simply as an expression of heartfelt nonobjective cosmic gratitude.

I propose that in the future we should regard the Eye of God as an optional form of consciousness, to be adopted as and when we feel the need of it or the desire for it. It is by no means the only option.

The Blissful Void

Not only in Buddhism but also in other religious traditions, the final goal of meditation and contemplative prayer is a state in which all imagery, difference, and form have disappeared, and the subject too is emptied out into void bliss. The texts compare this with sleep, with the snuffing out of a candle, with death, and with extinction. Since in our own society there are still many people who are distressed by the end of life after death, and who are irrationally afraid of death and the state of being dead, the discipline of the void can be of great therapeutic value. And there is no reason why we should not see meditation and contemplative prayer in purely secular and psychological terms, as forms of relaxation exercise. The warmth of relaxation and the warmth reported by the mystics are identical—in deep relaxation the capillary blood vessels widen, and the skin feels warmer.

The Blissful Void may be called the cool sublime. Standard discussions of the sublime usually begin with Burke and Kant, and in particular with the special kind of exaltation we feel when we contemplate the vastness of Nature (Kant's "mathematical sublime") or the might of Nature (Kant's "dynamical sublime": see 1987, pp. 103–23). Kant's teaching is that although the imagination may be defeated by the vastness of Nature, and although we may feel emotionally overwhelmed by the mighty force of Nature, our Reason is not defeated. Reason can and does number this vastness, and it describes the laws that these forces obey. So the Kantian sublime turns out in the end to be pride in our own rationality. I dislike that.

The cool sublime is quite different: indeed, it is the reverse of the Kantian sublime. In American abstract expressionist painting—for example, Barnett Newman's *Day One* (1951–52) —the canvas is unframed and, being a plain scarlet rectangle around twelve feet tall and four feet wide, almost resembles a swimming pool. The eye dives into it. The painting swallows one up. "The Sublime Is Now," declared Newman in his personal manifesto, and Mark C. Taylor comments: "This immediacy is the aesthetic version of the unitive experience that is the telos of negative theology" (1992, pp. 13–16). In my preferred terminology: the Blissful Void, the abstract sacred, the cool sublime, and the disappearance of the self into immanence, objectivity, and nothingness. I love that.

There is a further reason why we need the Discipline of the Void. In postmodern culture, after the end of the old metaphysics, nothing any longer has any assured and objective value, basis, or foundation. There is no fixed order of things out there. Everything is contingent, an outsideless flux of energies-read-as-signs that just pours out unceasingly and flits away. To repeat popular phrases already used, *This is it; this is all there is*—and now we are suddenly overcome with vertigo, because we have no idea whether to say that this fleeting life of ours has become infinitely important or infinitely *un*important. The juddering back and forth between weightiness and lightness is very difficult for many of us to bear right now, and I am suggesting that we should use the Discipline of the Void, meditation upon the underlying universal emptiness and nothingness, as a background against which to set and to see the flux of our life. The Blissful Void, *sunyata*, can thus replace the old metaphysical God, and give—to us Westerners in particular—a new and much-needed way of getting our life into perspective.

Solar Living

Modern knowledge suggests that the world consists of, and only of, an outpouring flux of minute energies. We are temporary aggregates of world-stuff. We maintain our existence for a while by reading world events as signs, expressing ourselves, and thereby also communicating with one another. (It will be noticed that, signs being general, all our communicative life depends upon a relation of the singular to the singular via the universal. To that extent, all of our communicative life is religious life.)

So we see the world as a flux of events-read-as-signs. World-stuff scatters and meanings disseminate unceasingly. There is nothing unchanging and nothing outside the flux. We should give up all ideas of so-called absolutes because there are none. We have no access to any objective order independent of ourselves. We contact only our own symbolic expressions, which briefly light upon and grasp at bits of world-stuff, before it slips away.

It follows that we ourselves are the only makers of meaning and value. Such meaning and value as we can descry in our life must be value that we have ourselves ascribed to it and projected into it. All the colors and "feels" of things are our own feelings, projected out. Ethics therefore must be solar. We no longer have any metaphysical reason or excuse for withholding ourselves. We should pour ourselves out as the sun does, identifying ourselves completely with the outpouring flux of all existence.

The great reason for doing this is that only by going out into symbolic self-expression can we get ourselves together. Within the human self there are always conflicting forces, but the sign has the marvelous property of being able to draw several different forces out at once, weaving them into relatively unified expression. So by self-exteriorization, self-outing, and self-shedding, we can make meaning and value—being so wonderfully duplicitous as we are, and as language is. We can live, we do live, by *out-lying*, by being true deceivers, by expressing ourselves and passing away. I call this *postsainthood*, meaning that though I make no sense in myself, being always a bundle of conflicting forces, I can make some sense in my expression, my spoken utterance, my work, and my lived life; provided, of course, that I understand that I must keep moving on, instantly leaving behind the expressed self that I am continually producing. Life can't be possessed or clutched at: we should pour ourselves out and pass on, without hesitation or regret. We can get ourselves together only by leaving ourselves behind. That is solarity—to live by dying all the time, heedless, like the sun and in the spirit of the Sermon on the Mount. Solar ethics is a radically emotivist and expressionist reading of the ethics of Jesus.

These three themes—the Eye of God, the Blissful Void, and Solar Living—between them comprise what is most worth preserving from the old religions, and perhaps offer a starting point for the religion of the future. We give up the notion of religion as a system of reassuring supernatural beliefs; and we adopt instead the idea of religion as a toolkit.

⹀THIRTEEN

Naturalism, Philosophy, and Religion

According to the archaeological record, the religious realm first became constituted as a distinct sphere of life around 3800 B.C. at Uruk. In chapter 3, I suggested that this was probably connected with the great need, in the early city-state, for a very strong central authority. Thereafter a dualistic cosmology steadily develops, contrasting the sacred and secular realms, religious and civil authority and law, the supernatural and natural worlds, and the human soul and body.

Today this very ancient dualism is finally coming to an end, and I have been proposing an interpretation, from a one-world or naturalistic point of view, both of what religion has been in the past and of what it may become in the future.

As an outlook, religious naturalism goes back at any rate to Spinoza. The young Hegelians—writers like Ludwig Feuerbach and Karl Marx—were very self-consciously resolving the religious world down into its secular basis already in the 1840s. But the strongest single influence upon modern religious naturalism has probably been Darwinism. After Darwin we were bound in the end to become committed to a nondualistic view of both the human being and the world.

But religious naturalism, it must be confessed, so far remains a minority view. Most people still associate religion with a separate sacred world, and with platonism, long-termism, transcendence, and supernaturalism. Such people are convinced that a painting can be religious only insofar as it can be read as an icon or sign that refers the viewer off the canvas, to an invisible spiritual realm beyond itself. In this view Barnett Newman's great scarlet rectangles cannot be religious paintings because their appeal is purely *on* the canvas, immediate and sensual. But, in my own terminology, Newman's great works are solar. They create an effect of ecstatic immanence in pure sensuous immediacy. They seek to fuse Eternity with Now; which, I say, is exactly what religion must henceforth do.

Nevertheless, it has to be admitted that most people remain obdurately supernaturalist in their understanding of religion. They will take some convincing that thoroughgoing naturalism, as a philosophical outlook, is now inescapable.

The proof, which is best given or at any rate suggested by Kant, is by way of showing that naturalism is equivalent to rationality. It is not possible to have a coherent practical view of life—especially in our own technological culture—except upon naturalistic assumptions. All our working ideas about what sorts of things may reasonably be expected to happen, or be regarded as probable, presuppose naturalism.

Imagine your car refuses to start, and you call in a mechanic. You watch him and answer his questions as he checks out what you both know is a finite list of possibilities. Not for one moment is either of you going to consider the theory that the car's failure to start has no cause, or is to be attributed to some supernatural agency.

Every day we make use of many complex technologies, confident that they have been rigorously tested and can be relied on to work. If one of them should turn out to be seriously faulty, we would not hesitate to go to law. Still worse, our technologies would be quite useless if their operation were really liable to disruption by supernatural agencies. The mechanic's job depends upon a presumption of naturalism. In the personal realm too, the same considerations apply. Imagine trying to write a play with half a dozen characters, one of whom has supernatural powers and may do anything whatever, without notice. It cannot be done: the play is unwritable. The whole framework of expectations about people and their likely behavior that we ordinarily live by has broken down. Anything may happen; and the result is chaos. We cannot calculate. We no longer know where we are.

In ordinary life we have to be naturalistic in outlook. Where a writer such as Shakespeare does have a supernatural apparatus, he cannot and does not weave it convincingly into the main plot. He pushes it out to the periphery, where it is used like the Chorus in a Greek play, to make comments and give clues. Shakespeare's real world of human interactions is a secular humanist narrative world, like the world of the two books of Samuel in the Hebrew Bible. It has to be.

Our assumptions are naturalistic because (for, roughly, Kantian reasons) we have to assume that space and time are continuous, with no gaps or sudden fast-forwards in them. We cannot apprehend anything except as an instance that falls under some general word or form of words, and we cannot understand any event or chain of events except as an instance that falls under some general rule or narrative pattern. In a word, our language itself is already committing us to classifying and theorizing things and events, just in order to get a hold of them; and the generality of language is the beginning of science.

If, then, in our daily tasks and social relationships we are always implicitly naturalistic in outlook, and if supernatural beliefs realistically understood never could be convincingly woven into the daily practice of life, how did supernaturalism ever develop? What was it *for?*

I have been suggesting that through its system of supernatural beliefs, a society represents to itself the ways that its language builds its world. When we relate myths and pass on supernatural beliefs, we are passing on coded instructions for world building, messages about values, recommended behavior patterns, and the like.

We cleave to, and we are chauvinistic about, our own particular body of supernatural beliefs and stories *because its distinctiveness is our identity*. It communicates, in coded form but very effectively nonetheless, our own distinctive vision of the world and form of life.

Because in the past it was generally felt to be essential to the maintenance of one's ethnic cultural tradition for all this material to be passed on without change and thoroughly assimilated by everyone, it was commonly taught and understood realistically—as if describing a really existing invisible supernatural world above. But today the globalization of our scientific theory, our technologies, and our communications has suddenly democratized naturalism everywhere.

The result is that tradition finds itself ironized, put in brackets, believed—and yet, surely, not *really* believed. We are exhorted and pressured to cleave to our own traditions, not because they can actually command our intellectual assent (they can't any more) but simply as a matter of ethnic loyalty and political duty. Judaism finds itself being converted into Zionism, and every other old religion similarly finds itself turning into a politicized, ethnonationalist, and Right-postmodernist version of itself. Intercommunal and interfaith conflicts have become endemic in many parts of the world.

Many people then find themselves caught in contradictions. The ways they are battling to defend and reaffirm their traditional faiths are not reversing, but rather are *accelerating* the loss of traditional religious values; and around the world the forces tending to liquidate traditional identities are much stronger than any attempts to conserve them can hope to be.

$\equiv$FOURTEEN

Globalization and the End of the Other

At the beginning of the twentieth century, it was still broadly the case that every human person and every human product had an obvious cultural provenance. Everyone and everything belonged somewhere—that is, had a background or context in which to be situated. Between them a panel of historians, anthropologists, museum curators, and the like would be able (or rather, would have been able, had they been armed with today's knowledge) very quickly to identify, with very little likelihood of error, just about anything presented to them. And in this context, note that to "identify" something means to give its home address, its place and date of origin within some historically evolving cultural tradition.

Each tradition, whether as small as a tribe or as large as a civilization, and even each period within a developing tradition, was a coherent totality with its own distinctive flavor or style that colored its every product, whether human, material, or ideal. You could not possibly confuse anything baroque with anything medieval, or anything Maya with anything Aztec, and so on. Of course there is such a thing as translation and of course there are analogies and homologies between cultures, but there remains an important sense in which cultures are incommensurable with one another. To each people the rest of the world seems profoundly Other, alien, strange, exotic, outside, and foreign. So much is this the case that many peoples regard contact with the Other as causing ritual defilement.

In 1900 only a few thinkers were beginning to see the implications of all this, thinkers such as Ernst Troeltsch and others influenced by German Idealism, and, most important, the French social theorist Emile Durkheim.

The argument now almost continues itself. The cultural totality within which a people lived was their creator. In it they lived and moved and had their being. It shaped everything they did and made. It had ultimate authority over them, to such an extent that everywhere men are expected to be ready to die for it. It had produced them and named them, giving them their identity, and it was therefore only fitting that they in return should be required to give it their unconditional allegiance, identifying it by its true and proper name, hallowing its sacred name, and being ready to fight in its name—the name of your One God, it is now clear, being equivalent to the unique and distinctive character (stamp or mark) and claims of the cultural totality or symbolic order to which you belong.

A fairly tidy scheme of thought is now in view. Gods are ethnic; each named god is covenanted to a particular people whose god he is; your god's function is to *badge* the cultural totality within which you live and to which you owe allegiance; every theology conveys a host of social messages, because the religious law laid down by your named god is a set of framework rules for producing your people's version of the symbolic order; and finally, your god indwells you at least in the sense that (poetically speaking) the national spirit indwells each person. More exactly, you have very specific cultural inscriptions written all over you. All your speech and all your behaviors are culturally molded and legible. That is the *literally* "literal" meaning of divine indwelling: that the law is *written* on our hearts—meaning that we are inwardly formed and made by the sign system within which we function.

So the normal and happy state of affairs in the human world is one in which the tribe, the language group, the nation-state, or whatever is internally at peace, united in worship of its own god, and externally is always militarily prepared to defend itself against the encircling Others. The happiest state of all is a state of open war, a time when it is well known that the crime rate, the suicide rate, and mental illness rates tumble. People are united in directing all their hatred and aggression externally against the Other, and so are deeply at peace among and within themselves.

In the last book of the Old Testament, God is reported as saying: "Is not Esau Jacob's brother? Yet I have loved Jacob but I have hated Esau" (Malachi 1:2). For there to be choice, there must also be rejection; for there to be love, there must also be hatred; for there to be a We there must also be a They, and the line that includes some must always exclude Others. Separation and not mixture is natural to human groups, and war is normal, not peace. In Israel recently there was an interesting coincidence of opposites when ultraconservative Jews and fundamentalist Palestinians, Jacob and Esau, were united in opposition to peace with each other. The former group brought about the assassination of Yitzak Rabin, and the latter the assassination of busloads of Israeli civilians. The two groups were at one in regarding separation and war as the normal and happy state of relations between them. Such is conservatism.

And such was pretty much the state of affairs in the *Europe des patries* of 1900. But conversely, by the end of the twentieth century, it has become clear that the process of rapid cultural globalization now under way presents a profound challenge to all our ancestral ways of thinking, ways of feeling, and ways of constructing our various worlds. What has been happening in Northern Ireland, in Bosnia, in Israel/Palestine, and in many other places has been more than enough to convince a fair-minded person that we simply cannot afford any longer our old tribalisms, our old ethnonationalisms, and our old religions. They are all of them hatred machines. They unite only by dividing, binding people together in fellowship only by directing their aggression externally against the demonized Other. The heretic, the apostate, the heathen, the infidel, the enemy of God, the dirty foreigner—all this is a vocabulary we can no longer afford. The world has become too small and crowded to permit the use of such language.

Interestingly, our great multinational corporations and systems of communication and exchange already practice a kind of global political correctness. They rather deliberately bracket out, set aside, any consideration of gender, nationality, race, color, creed. A worker is a worker and a customer is a customer, regardless. It is conventional to criticize the multinationals for being mobile, rootless, anonymous, and interested only in profit, but I'm pointing out that it is *precisely these features* that make them morally superior to our old locally based national and religious identities. Being mobile and global, they cannot afford to operate by generating and excluding an Other, and they have therefore had to find a new basis for communal loyalty.

How do they do it? When the great multinational companies and exchanges are called virtual countries, people wonder how they manage to command the loyalty of those who work for them. They are not bound by the traditional ties of blood, land, and religion. They are a kind of entity that has been able to appear only after the end of the old agriculture-based type of civilization, and that seems radically secular by its standards. The multinational company shows that a flourishing human society doesn't need to be bound to a particular stretch of land given to the founding fathers by God, doesn't need to be of one blood, and doesn't need to be bound together in worship of the God of the fathers. More than that, it doesn't need to define itself vis-à-vis an encircling, threatening Other, and it therefore does not need a guarded, continuous frontier separating like a skin its interior from the exterior.

It is very postmodern suddenly to realize that we no longer actually need roots, identity, stability, or a provenance. We can do without all those things. Me, I don't want them anymore. I prefer to be without identity. I'd like to belong to no ethnic group, and to have no Other. They call me a nihilist: but I'm beginning to feel at ease, *at home* in nihilism. There are those who hope to restore the good old days by turning Islam into a new demonized Other; but quite apart from the fact that outside the traditional territory of Islam there is now a very large and growing Muslim diaspora, which is itself destined to become postmodernized, the attempt to restore our own sense of identity by victimizing Islam is in any case unnecessary and unprofitable. We simply don't need the old social and religious categories and ways of thinking, and have no reason for attempting at this time to reinstate them. We do not need them in order to create community, and, curiously, we do not need them in order to be ourselves.

The postmodernization of persons, of cultural products, and of goods goes back to the beginning of the twentieth century. Already in connection with figures like Nellie Melba and Charlie Chaplin, we see both that they were made ubiquitous by new technologies and that they were in themselves somewhat nomadic and elusive. We are not too sure we know just where they were born, where they died, what their nationality was, and what were their real names. Does it matter? And something similar in due course gets to be true of thousands of twentieth-century figures, just as it is also true of more and more goods, commodities, and ways of doing things. As the technologies get to be more and more powerful, everything is multiplied endlessly in order to become immediately accessible to everyone. Otherness disappears in the infinite free-associating hospitability of mediaspace. When I have read a shelf of novels about the lost world of East European Jewry by I. L. Peretz, S. Y. Agnon, Isaac Bashevis Singer, and others, then that world belongs to me as much as to the Jews themselves. Why not? I'm as close to it as they are. The new globalized culture breaks down the barriers of space and time, Otherness and Difference, and returns everything into the superabundant virtual present.

The old sort of life, rooted in place and time, land and kinship, and exclusive national and religious allegiances, is already largely lost. Already we know too much and have become too plural. Various sorts of ethnonationalists and religious fundamentalists may think they can turn back the clock; but they cannot. Already reality has become a web of communication, an outpouring, outsideless flux of signs that has caught us up and carried us away with it. It is, and we are with it, foundationless and goalless. It isn't going anywhere, nor are we. There is such a torrent of little meanings that there can no longer be any great overarching Meaning of it All.

So what happens to religion and morality in these strange new conditions? We go *solar*.

⊒FIFTEEN

The End of Morality and the Return of Ethics

The rapid decline of the old religions, I have been saying, is linked with the passing of the old agriculture-based civilizations and the very specific types of political structure and religious ideology they produced. It has recently been predicted that by the year 2000 half the human race, and by the year 2025 two-thirds of all humanity, will be city dwellers hooked into the new global culture.

We have seen that, in order to get itself going in the first place, the early city-state had to set up a very strong sacred center of authority and focus of allegiance. This developed in time into a clear dualism between the sacred and profane worlds: God and king, temple and palace, heaven and earth, the supernatural and natural worlds. The god in his temple bound his holy people to their holy land and the cycles of human days, years, and lifetimes into the cyclical rhythms of the cosmos. By their exclusive allegiance to the god and to the specific version of the symbolic order that he had given them, his holy people distinguished themselves from the encircling (threatening, unclean) Others around them. A certain ethnic pride in their own separateness and unique identity thus compensated them for the stringent disciplinary demands of religious law.

At the peak of its development, the whole system generated very large scale narrative cosmologies and systems of doctrine. When, during the so-called Axial Age (circa −800 to +600 of the Common Era), a new concern about the individual's journey to personal salvation arose and had to be built into the system, each individual's life history was also taken up into a lengthy narrative. God had (so you hoped) predestined you for salvation from all eternity, and your earthly life was but a moment in comparison with what would come after it. It might take 90,000 lifetimes for you to become a Buddha, 500,000 years of Purgatory to make you fit for Heaven. Final blessedness was thus both infinitely important and almost infinitely far away. Yet every act in your life might in principle have a direct bearing on your personal attainment of your final goal. Accordingly, elaborate systems of religious law were developed, with the aim of producing a morally unified life properly oriented toward the attainment of its end. Morality thus came to be seen on the legal model: it was ascetical, disciplinary, and very long-termist.

The single most impressive intellectual achievement of the old order was Plato's metaphysics, the twenty-odd founding principles of which sustained the old order until the Enlightenment. But as agricultural civilization has gradually been replaced by our new science-based industrial civilization, so a line of philosophers running from Hume and Kant up to Nietzsche and the young Derrida has simultaneously been at work dismantling Plato's entire platform plank by plank.

So what happens next? Interestingly, the old faiths were not only very large-scale and cosmological; they also developed, in dialectical opposition to the large-scale vision, a highly focused and short-term vision centered around the individual's desire to experience salvation not at the end of time but *now*. The contrast here is roughly that between dogmatism and existentialism, or between metaphysics and its deconstruction; between the cosmic grand narrative and the sudden conversion of soul or flash of enlightenment (*satori*) by which the individual momentarily seizes blessedness.

The grand-narrative vision sees the way to salvation as a lengthy pilgrimage, an arduous ascent or a disciplined purging that passes through many stages. To sustain us on the journey we will need a great disciplinary institution that teaches us all the right things to believe and all the right rules to keep. During the great journey that is history, we regularly remind ourselves of the founding events that began our journey and the hope of glory awaiting us at its end. The life story of the individual is thus given meaning by being taken up into the larger social and cosmic story. My own life story, from baptism to death, Purgatory and Heaven, fits into the long march of the Church, militant, expectant, and triumphant, which in turns fits into a cosmic narrative that runs from eternity to eternity via Creation, Fall, and Redemption.

Today, however, the whole cosmological or grand narrative side of religion has totally collapsed. We know, if we know anything, that there is no rationally ordered scheme of things out there, no grand-narrative meaning-of-life already laid on for our lives to be fitted into. We know, if we know anything, that there isn't literally any supernatural order, and there is not literally any life after death. This is all there is, and, as everyone knows, when you're dead you're dead.

And what *is* "this"? There is and there is only an outpouring, continuously renewed flux of minute world events, of which we are simply parts. We can apprehend *the* world as and only as *our* world, a world colored by our own feelings, formed by our language, and structured by our theories. There is no real world in the sense of a ready-made cosmos, with rationality, meanings, and values antecedently laid on for us. What we see before us is not a naked-yet-finished world ready-made for us, because we never see a naked world. What we see is always and only a world *view*, a construction of things that we have ourselves evolved over the centuries and millennia past. We see a world highly made up, fully clothed, and every bit of the way we see what we see has a history. Both on the largest scale and in the smallest detail, what we perceive is a humanly appropriated world.

In our hearts we all know that that is how things are. In which case the spread-out, grand-narrative cosmological sort of religion is either dead or at the very least in need of drastic revision and reinterpretation. As for the religious emphasis, it now comes to be placed on the short-term vision. Not the large-scale doctrine-system and moral code, but the telescoped, contracted vision, which is sometimes called an "ethic" in the archaic sense and otherwise may be spoken of as a form of consciousness, as a spirituality, as a way of life, and so forth.

What survives of the old religions, then, is a small number of tricks and techniques of religious existence: ways of being a self and of relating oneself to the whole of which one is a part. These tricks can help us to love life and live well: that, now, is religion. I have described three such tricks. The Eye of God is the trick of relating oneself to oneself via the universal, seeing oneself and one's expressed life as if through God's eyes. This is what remains valuable in the idea of God. The Blissful Void is the trick of relaxing completely, slowing oneself and one's passions down until the self is, as it were, dispersed into the fleeting insubstantial emptiness of all existence. You must learn to experience nihilism as levity, lightness. The strange unexpected happiness this brings is a wonderful deliverance from the fear of death, loss, and suffering. Solar Living is the trick of casting oneself unreservedly into the flux of existence, spending oneself, living as hard as one can, burning without being afraid of burnout.

This state of being lost in life I call "ecstatic immanence."

Such were the traditional—or partly traditional—techniques of religious existence that were mentioned earlier. Their practice is ethics. A further group will be described shortly under the heading of "poetical theology." Meanwhile, a crucial point is now to be developed: they are all voluntary, and the setting in which they are to be appropriated and practiced is *innocent*.

SIXTEEN

Innocent Religion?

You may well be skeptical about the severely reconstructed notion of religion that I am putting forward. It seems to be religion without metaphysics, religion without creed, religion no longer focused around a power center outside ourselves, religion without a structure of authority, and religion without a gathered community of people who are very conscious of a clear line between themselves, the elect, and the rest of humanity.

In place of all that, I am offering only religion as a toolkit, a small set of attitudes and techniques, by practicing which we can grow in self-knowledge (the Eye of God), learn to accept the transience and insubstantiality of ourselves and everything else (the Blissful Void), and learn to say a wholehearted yes to life (Solar Living). Another item is yet to be added: it is the *Poetical Theology*, which is (briefly) a license to make whatever new use we can of the surviving scraps of vocabulary, ritual, and symbolism that are available to us.

My suspicion is that you will regard this revision of the

concept of religion as being very reductionist in spirit. And why do you think that? Because for thousands of years we have been accustomed to extreme religious authoritarianism and disciplinarianism. Even to this day people are troubled by the thought that there is a real ready-made cosmos out there. They think the world is like a boarding school or a penitentiary, a huge disciplinary institution, a place of probation with *both* built-in moral rules of behavior *and* a built-in apparatus that will in the long run see that all the rules are enforced. Eventually, your sins will find you out. Realistic theism has classically pictured God as an infinite spirit, all-powerful, all-seeing, recording everything and intensely, really *intensely*, judgmental. Before God and by God's standard of absolute perfection, every single one of us is always in the wrong, at all times and everywhere. So for a large part of humanity, all of life has been clouded by fear and anxiety for thousands of years.

The aftereffects of all this cosmological terrorism are still with us. For example, the largest and most powerful religious organizations today, whether Christian or Islamic, seem to attract people precisely because they are authoritarian. They appear to confirm the widespread tendency simply to equate religiousness with glad submission to domination; and, within them, revivalist movements that are even more authoritarian continue to appear. Spiritual power, it seems, always demands more and more of itself—more puritanism, more repression, more cruelty. In this way the virus of the lust for spiritual power has turned religions of redemption into machines for destroying the human spirit. And in the new religious movements, the "NRMs" that are often popularly described as cults, exactly the same characteristics are still appearing, over and over again.

It may indeed be that an overwhelming and annihilating system of religious terrorism was needed in order to discipline the hunter-gatherers into becoming good citizens of the first state societies. It may even be that a terroristic religious ideology was still necessary for the sake of social order even as late as the sixteenth and seventeenth centuries.

John Calvin and his friends evidently thought so. In Geneva, on October 16, 1551, Jerome Bolsec publicly criticized the doctrine of double predestination: "those who posit an eternal decree in God by which he has ordained some to life and the rest to death make of him a Tyrant, and in fact an idol, as the pagans made of Jupiter." Bolsec was evidently an early nonrealist, a critic of the objectification of God for the sake of power. Inevitably, he was arrested on the spot by Calvin's people (see Parker 1975, pp. 111ff).

Today, religious terrorism ought to be unendurable, and Nietzsche's great doctrine of the "innocence of becoming" expresses the happiness and the sense of rebirth we feel when we finally get the old fear, melancholy, and spiritual sadomasochism out of our psychology. We are *not* accountable, we are *not* chronically in the wrong, and there is no reason whatsoever for thinking that the whole of our existence is somehow blighted:

> *No one* is accountable for existing at all, or for being constituted as he is, or for living in the circumstances and surroundings in which he lives. The fatality of his nature cannot be disentangled from the fatality of all that which has been and will be. He is *not* the result of a special design, a will, a purpose; he is *not* the subject of an attempt to attain to an "ideal of man" or an "ideal of happiness" or an "ideal of morality"—it is absurd to want to *hand over* his nature to some purpose or other. *We* invented the concept "purpose": in reality purpose is *lacking*. . . . One is necessary, one is a piece of fate, one belongs to the whole, one *is* in the whole—there exists nothing which could judge, measure, compare, condemn our being, for that would be to judge, measure, compare, condemn the whole. . . . *But nothing exists apart from the whole!* That no one is any longer made accountable, that the kind of being mani-

fested cannot be traced back to a *causa prima*, that the world is a unity neither as sensorium nor as spirit, *this alone is the great liberation*—thus alone is the *innocence* of becoming restored. . . . The concept "God" has hitherto been the greatest *objection* to existence. . . . We deny God; in denying God, we deny accountability: only by doing *that* do we redeem the world. [1968, p. 54; italics in original]

Just as the best way to conquer Satan is to give up the belief in Satan, so the quick way to save the world is to give up believing all the ugly old doctrines that made us feel that we are miserable sinners, and that life as a whole is unsatisfactory.

I want to make the point even more strongly than Nietzsche does, because we should now be even more language-minded and humanistic in our thinking than he was. For us, there is only *us* and *all this*. There is our language, the selves our language gives us to be, and the world our language gives us to inhabit. Belief in hidden powers is *exactly* as absurd and superstitious as the belief that there are a lot of invisible words in the dictionary that somehow interfere with the meanings and the movements of the visible words.

Nietzsche eloquently celebrates the restoration of the innocence of the transient world of Becoming. Why should we not restore the innocence of religion? Why should there not be religion that is free of illusion, untruth, and power worship?

⅀SEVENTEEN

The Poetical Theology

Two centuries ago, in the early years of the Romantic move-ment, there was a hope expressed in some quarters that reli-gion, having died as dogma, might be reborn as art. In a notebook of about 1804 William Blake has left a vivid—if unpolished—example of this idea. He writes as one for whom the poetical imagination is a numinous world-building power that can never be supplanted or dethroned, either by the mockery of rationalist critics or by scientific theories:

> *Mock on, mock on, Voltaire, Rousseau!*
> *Mock on, mock on—'Tis all in vain!*
> *You throw the sand against the wind,*
> *And the wind blows it back again*
>
> *And every sand becomes a gem*
> *Reflected in the beams divine;*
> *Blown back they blind the mocking eye,*
> *But still in Israel's paths they shine.*

The atoms of Democritus
And Newton's particles of light
Are sands upon the Red Sea shore,
Where Israel's tents do shine so bright.

As the Romantics saw it, the leading ideas of the Enlightenment had been as damaging to art as to religion, and for much the same reasons. Since Descartes, the demand had been all for a thoroughly demystified world view, expressed in the clearest possible terms. True sentences must either report empirical facts or precisely state the logical relations between clear and distinct ideas. In the older culture the world had been held together by language, that is, by a complex symbolic network of analogies, correspondences, and great narratives. But the triumph of the newer ideal meant that there was no longer any room for the strong, world-building uses of language. Tragic drama, epic poetry, and the great tradition in religious art simply ceased. Under the new cultural regime works of art were required to be pleasing to reason by the correctness of their proportions, and pleasing to our feelings by being charming and decorative. Above all art must please by being true to Nature; but it could not be seen as changing reality. Nature and Reason always came first, and art's place was only to follow them. It could not lead the way.

In such a world view, language is always seen as coming second. Language merely copies or tracks a ready-made order of things. And this new, radically simplified, and literal understanding of what language is and may be used to do had an effect upon religion that was as drastic as its effects upon art. People lost their old feeling for the way myths, rituals, and symbols interlink various aspects of the world to build up a coherent vision of life and to structure social relationships. They could no longer see either the imagination or language as being truly creative. The imagination, having long been viewed as Satan's gateway to the mind, was associated with deception, illusion, seduction, and untruth. Only God could create reality just by using language, and his work was not to be improved or corrected by human agency. There was only one case in which a human act could be spoken of as a pure act of creation, and, significantly, it had to do with law and politics, not art. It was the case familiar to lawyers, where a sovereign person or body creates a new status or institution just by saying so. In those days the most godlike thing on the human scene was thought to be absolute power.

Against this background—legalism, literalism, and the Enlightenment's extremely simplified vision of the world—religious beliefs were sorted out under two headings. There was *rational theology*, which consisted of a body of universal truths that could be established just by philosophical argument; and there was *revealed theology*, which consisted of a body of propositions that were "above reason" and were to be believed on authority, by faith.

If the propositions of revealed theology are indeed above reason, must they not also be beyond our understanding? Some called them mysterious, or even contrary to reason. But the early Enlightenment was also a late Baroque period, with a heavy emphasis upon sovereign authority; and authority had its own reasons for wanting unconditional assent to clearly understood doctrines, without any twisting of their meaning. It thus became politically necessary to hold that the propositions of faith are clear and plain. So King James I of England demands in *His Majesty's Declaration* (1628) that the Articles of Religion must be understood and accepted in their "literal and grammatical sense," which is their "true, usual and literal meaning," their "plain and full meaning." Lawyer-like, the king insists that there is such a thing as literal meaning, and he puts it first.

In the Middle Ages, when the monks distinguished the literal from the allegorical, mystical, and other senses of a scriptural passage, they did not by any means invariably presume the superior honesty and moral authority of the literal meaning. When, for example, scripture orders animal sacrifice, we are not expected to go and perform one. But after the Reformation both churches and princes had become heavily involved in the use of law to control doctrine, enforcing just one interpretation as alone acceptable, and prohibiting others. The lawyers' type of literalism became dominant, perhaps especially among those influenced by Calvinism. The propositions of faith were to be accepted as realistically or literally true descriptions of supernatural states of affairs and goings-on, and were to be believed as a matter of legal and moral duty simply upon the authority of the Revealer. As for the Revealer, he is God or Christ, revealing saving truth through such channels as the Bible, the Church, the pope— and even (as it later came to be held) personal religious experience.

These doctrines effectively destroyed theology as an epic subject and a subject of major cultural importance, because they left the theologian with no important job to do except advocacy. If Tradition is already perfect and whole, if the Bible is inerrant, if dogma is immutable, if the pope is infallible, and if only one interpretation is lawful, then there can be no question of reinterpreting, reimagining, reinventing, or reminting religious belief. The System already knows all the answers. The theologian's task is merely to give us grounds for assenting to the Truth, by demonstrating the strength of the credentials of its mouthpiece and by showing the error of all its opponents and critics.

It is true that the philosophers—and in particular Hume and Kant—demolished the old rational theology, and it is true that the Deists and other rationalist critics fatally undermined the credentials of revelation; but it is still more important to understand the extent to which, early in the Enlightenment, the great tradition in Christianity destroyed itself by its own disastrous infatuation with literalism and the use of pure power to control language. Today's exhausted Roman authoritarianism and vacuous Protestant fundamentalism are the long-term consequences. When language is policed too tightly, religion slowly dies.

As we said earlier, the Romantic movement arose at a time when the Great Tradition had indeed died, both in religion and in art. The Romantics did not relish the prospect— already coming into view—of a clockwork culture of mechanized production and bureaucratic regulation. They dreamed of a cultural revival led by the creative imagination in a way that would fully synthesize religion and art, and build a new world.

Already within the tradition there were a few scraps available to the Romantics that might encourage them in their great enterprise. Within the Jewish Torah a well-known passage finds no difficulty at all in simply equating artistic inspiration with divine inspiration (Exodus 31:1–5). More important to the Romantics and to many of their successors was the originally religious character of the theater, especially in Greece. The grand revolutionary project of a simultaneous relaunch of art and religion *as each other* had an unimpeachable pedigree in Greek tragedy. And, linked with this, there was also the notion of the poetical theology.

Briefly to recall the source of this idea, Augustine (1945, vol. 1, pp. 178–95) quotes the late-Roman writer Varro as distinguishing among the *philosophical theology*, which is simply the truth as it is known to philosophers and is taught by them in their schools; the *civil theology*, which is the established state religion whose rites are performed in the temples; and the *poetical theology* displayed in the work of poets and dramatists as they rework the old myths about the gods. Its place of enactment is usually the theater.

There is a certain amount of quibbling over words here, because the philosophical theology may alternatively be called *natural* or *physical*, and the poetical theology may also be called *mythical* or *fabulous*. But that is by the way: Augustine's own purpose is of course to drive the poetical theology underground, and to keep it firmly repressed for the next thousand years. Having invented his own epic narrative theology, Augustine does not want it to have any rivals. He wants a monopoly. To make Christian faith into a powerful and effective system of social control, it must be objectified as The Faith, defined dogmatically, believed realistically, and enforced legally. Every totalitarian system justifiably hates and fears the free play of the creative imagination as a deadly threat to its power, and a deep suspicion of art has become so entrenched, especially in the Christian and Muslim traditions, that ordinary believers have internalized it. To this day artistic license in the treatment of a sacred subject matter angers them more than anything else—as Salman Rushdie, Martin Scorsese, and many others have found.

After Augustine, then, the poetical theology could not easily reenter Christianity directly. The control of religious meaning by power was too strong. But it could and did enter indirectly, by way of the very strikingly effective Renaissance revival and exploitation of classical mythology. Since the Church had always hated the gods of Greece and Rome, it was not going to object that they were now being blasphemed. And since it had always said that the gods were vain deceits, it did not object to their being treated nonrealistically, as allegories or mythical personifications of human moral values.

Having therefore a free hand, and being assured by Ovid himself that everything in the sacred world is prone to sudden metamorphoses, the artists were free to take up and exploit the surviving literary and artistic remnants of classical antiquity. Using this vocabulary they built a new order—a new way of seeing, a new attitude to the senses and to this world, a new vision of landscape and of the human body, a new awareness of the passions and of role play, a new sense of human life as theater—in short, the early modern world. They showed that a poetical theology can be the instrument by which a culture transforms and rejuvenates itself.

The next question is clearly whether Christianity itself

might in turn be given the same treatment. In retrospect it is now possible to recognize a postmodernist and poetical strand already within Western Christianity going back as far as the later Middle Ages. It shows up whenever a religious theme is treated with a touch, or more than a touch, of irony, satire, self-mockery, or playfulness. It shows up when the normal hierarchies and valuations are mocked and reversed at feasts such as Carnival and Christmas. It shows up when believers consciously allow themselves to overelaborate their own myths—just in fun.

Such a playful type of poetical theology was tolerable and tolerated precisely because it does not undermine but rather confirms the authority of the normality that it mocks. In the period of the great theological crisis (1780–1840), however, it became clear to the leading spirits in Germany and neighboring lands that Christianity really *had* died as dogma. Kant and Hegel, the French Revolution, and the Young Hegelians D. F. Strauss, Feuerbach, and Karl Marx between them had seen to that. In which case Christianity might now be available for transformation by a thoroughgoing poetical theology. It could perhaps be reborn as and in art.

What we got was unfortunately something rather less than that. We got neomedievalism and the Gothic revival: Christianity abolished and replaced by a consuming mood of yearning nostalgia for itself—in short, the modern Church. We got Richard Wagner and the *Festspeilhaus* at Bayreuth. And we got the commercial and industrial culture of the nineteenth century. But we did not get the sort of rebirth of religion and art *as each other* of which a few of the Romantics had dreamed.

From the 1880s matters improved, and there was a certain revival of the Romantic project. The best young artists were becoming confident enough to repudiate the Academies, and formal secessions took place in Munich and Berlin in 1892 and in Vienna in 1897. Art was beginning explicitly to dissociate itself from the established social and cultural order. It was not enough merely to please existing taste, or to dignify and embellish the existing social order. Art had a higher task than that. Art was to become utopian and redemptive. The painter's task was to change the way we see the world, thereby to change the world, and to change human beings themselves. The Modern Movement was being born, and it had strongly religious ambitions from the outset.

Here the account I would prefer to give differs somewhat from that given by Mark C. Taylor in *Disfiguring* (1992b). For Taylor, the principal religious strand in Modernism is the movement toward abstraction and the Negative Theology. His account therefore runs from Cézanne through Cubism to Mondrian, Malevich, and Kandinsky, and then on to the American Abstract Expressionism of Pollock, Rothko, and Newman. The painting story then ends very pessimistically, with Anselm Kiefer. In architecture, rather similarly, Taylor's story runs from Oscar Wagner and Adolf Loos through Le Corbusier, the Bauhaus, and on to Philip Johnson. And yes, that is indeed one strand in Modernism; but there is another story, one that begins in the late 1880s with, for example, van Gogh and the School of Pont-Aven (Gaugin, Bernard, Anquetin), and then runs through a variety of symbolists and Fauves (for example, Denis, Derain, Matisse, Vlaminck) and so on to *der Blaue Reiter* and German Expressionism. A number of these artists had, like Chagall, a personal background in biblical painting and peasant life, to which they often return. They are, in my jargon, *solar*. They see the world as outpouring energetic process. They are highly emotivist or expressivist. They love the strongest sunlight and the most blazing colors. They practice a form of extravertive mysticism, believing that through painting it may be possible, in William Blake's words, to "cleanse the doors of perception and see everything as it is, infinite." Favorite sources of imagery for them include the circus, paradise, the jungle, and dreams.

In 1994 I first published the phrase *ecstatic immanence* in connection with a religious outlook of this type, only to find Robert S. Corrington of Drew University coining *ecstatic naturalism* in the same year. Older phrases include Carlyle's *natural supernaturalism* and, from the 1960s, *superrealism*.

Modern painting, then, in its great days, around 1885 to 1970, was pursuing something very close to the religious agenda set out in this book (see Kandinsky 1977). The Blissful Void is seen in the movement toward the abstract sublime and minimalism. Solar Ethics is the concern of the Fauvist and Expressionist traditions. As for the Eye of God, the classic method of pursuing this style of spirituality in painting is through a series of self-portraits, a genre of which there have been many fine modern exponents.

What was the philosophical rationale for the confidence of the Romantics—and later, the Moderns—that by poetry and painting the world could be changed? Undoubtedly, the answer lies chiefly in the history of German philosophy. Allan Megill has usefully suggested the term *aestheticism* for a philosophical outlook that attempts "to expand the aesthetic to embrace the whole of reality" (1985, p. 2). This means not just that we only ever get hold of the world indirectly, and through the movement of the signs and symbols in which we seek to represent it, but, more strongly, that the spontaneously creative motion of signs and symbols produces *us too*. Language speaks *us*—meaning, I think, that we ourselves are by no means fully in control of, or even conscious of, the creative and productive motion of language within ourselves. It makes us; it makes the world: it makes and unmakes all things.

Fully developed aestheticism is most clearly stated by Nietzsche: "The world is a work of art that gives birth to itself" (1968, #796). The later Heidegger continues in the same vein. But the germ of these doctrines is already to be found in Kant—or, at least, in Kant as the Romantics read him. In Kant's "transcendental idealism" our knowledge is not a copy or representation of a ready-made external world, independent of the mind. On the contrary, the raw chaotic stuff presented to us becomes a formed and ordered world only in and through our comprehension of it. Our knowing is itself a complex creative activity, in a manner of which we are ordinarily quite unaware. (To give a modern parallel, we are not consciously aware of what goes on in the visual cortex, but a great deal evidently does go on there.) Kant also gives a special place in our knowledge to the work of the imagination, which must synthesize and unify the manifold that is presented to it. And Kant further impressed his Romantic contemporaries by the way he recognized the autonomy of the aesthetic in his *Critique of Judgment*.

In a word, the Romantics could easily read Kant as teaching that the world is created, or creates itself as world, in and through our knowledge of it, and in a way of which we are largely unconscious.

Nietzsche's hyberbolic Romanticism makes the will-to-power pretty much what Freud called libido. It is an outpouring excessive life-energy coming out into expression as sex, or as artistic creativity, or as play: "Making music is another way of making children" (#800). Nietzsche repeatedly insists that religious excitement and sexual excitation are very nearly one and the same, in which case one is surprised to find him so reluctant to consider the project of a poetical theology. Why should we not see our great religious traditions as being like art traditions?

In fact, it is only quite recently that we have felt able openly and explicitly to describe theologies, systematized statements of religious faith, as products of the creative imagination (for example, Kaufman 1975, 1993; Cupitt 1984). But we should be cautious at this point. One should not simply reverse the popular theology, and instead of "God made us in his own image," say "We made God in our own image"; for that is an oversimplification. Nietzsche, in a note already quoted, talks about the "work of art where it appears without an artist, e.g. as body, as organization." It is quite possible for a complex cultural formation to appear and eventually to pass away, without any particular individual being conscious of having personally designed it or having abolished it. (Wittgenstein makes a similar point about language games. Suddenly we notice that a particular game is no longer being played, a particular word has fallen into disuse because, somehow, it ceased to do any useful job. But very often we do not plan these changes: we just find that they have happened.) So one might say that God brought himself into being in and through the development of our language about him; but in recent centuries he has withdrawn as we have found ourselves needing less and less to speak of him.

As God has faded we have found ourselves gradually becoming able to speak of the theologian as a creative worker and gaining the courage to borrow from other traditions. We should stop speaking of other religious traditions as if they are alive and in good health. They are not: they are all declining very rapidly, like Christianity, and all are available to be looted of whatever they possess that may be useful to us in the future.

I am suggesting that we can and should now be uninhibited and eclectic in creating new religious meanings, practices, and narratives out of the materials available to us. The poetical theology will fiction and refiction our religion, tell and retell the old stories. What will make it a *theology* will be its use in helping us to see ourselves and our life with a greater clarity of moral vision, in helping us to be "easy, going" about the transience of everything, and in showing us how to live ardently.

ᴇEIGHTEEN

World Religion

All around the world now, schoolchildren are studying much the same syllabus: English, mathematics, science, and technology. Transport, communications, the financial and commodity markets, and even news and entertainment are almost completely globalized. Everywhere, cities contain much the same range of institutions—the bank, the hospital, the power station, the broadcasting station, the university, the high-rise office block—all employing much the same range of skills and resting on much the same bodies of knowledge. A single continuous world culture is very rapidly consolidating itself.

This new world culture is secular and increasingly transnational. Within it we hear the language of nationalism and of religion only from those people who most fear and are trying the hardest to resist the changes that are taking place. They fear oblivion, because they suspect that they and everything they have stood for—their world, their beliefs and values, their identity—will shortly vanish unlamented and be completely forgotten. In the hope of confirming and prolonging their distinct identity, they beat the drums, close ranks, and adopt a permanently embattled posture. Yet for how long can they hold out? In the Indian subcontinent Hindus may battle against Buddhists in Sri Lanka, and against Sikhs and Muslims in the northwest. But in the great territories between, India is beginning to modernize rapidly, and the time will come when the voice of the markets demanding peace and stability will be louder than the voice of the old gods demanding war.

It is very curious that God and Mammon should have changed places ethically. Mammon is an internationalist. He wants people to be healthy and well educated. He wants peace and stability, progress and universal prosperity. By contrast, God (especially in the Middle East) appears to have become a Moloch who demands ignorance, poverty, and war. The Four Horsemen of the Apocalypse may be very bad for human beings, but they are very good for God.

Will there be, can there ever be, a new globalized *world* religion that does *not* work by dividing humanity into a We and a They, but expresses an emergent collective consciousness of the unity of the whole human race with our common world?

A century or two ago, people still thought this might be possible. Various Western thinkers since Leibniz have been impressed by the strong moral solidarity of Asian societies, and since Schopenhauer many have also been impressed by the analogies between the histories of Indian and Western philosophy. Until as recently as the generation of W. E. Hocking, Aldous Huxley, and Arnold Toynbee, there were those who hoped for a religious unification of the human race under the aegis of something like the perennial philosophy.

That approach has now been abandoned. Hocking's well-known report *Rethinking Missions* (1932), which advocated an (approximately) syncretistic approach to the Asian traditions, was sharply rebutted by Hendrik Kraemer in *The Christian*

Message in a Non-Christian World (1938), and, more generally, *all* the great religions have subsequently chosen the path
of difference and separation rather than the path of syn-
cretism. More important, with the end of both metaphysical
realism and moral realism, the postmodern world has become quite markedly postphilosophical. Without any commonly understood philosophical vocabulary, the traditional
religions of humankind can now survive only as fundamentalisms—which is what they have largely become.

What would seem to follow for the rest of us is thoroughgoing permissive pluralism. If indeed there is no One Great
Truth out there to serve as the basis for a future worldwide
common human religious consciousness, and if indeed there
is no One True Morality out there either, then perhaps
Nietzsche is right and our truths are indeed merely "those
illusions without which we cannot live." What is true for any
person is what gives that person a feeling of enhanced
strength, confidence, and vitality (see Nietzsche 1968,
nos. 533–35), and there may be any number of such subjective truths. In which case, surely, one should be happy to see
the three thousand or so New Religious Movements, the
thousand or so New Age groups, and the hundreds of sects of
the various major faiths that are all flourishing, teeming, in
Western countries today. If their beliefs work out well for
them, then their beliefs are true for them; and since there is
no independent Truth out there, and all of us are entirely
free to build our worlds in the ways that seem best to us, we
have no basis for calling other people's worlds irrational. Let
a hundred flowers bloom! The old mirroring type of rationality, which consisted in the conformity of the human mind
with the way things are out there, is dead. There *is* no ready-
made, or antecedently fixed, way that things are. In any view,
surely, the world has to be interpretatively plastic enough for
a large number of widely different religious faiths and cultural perspectives each to work out happily for its own adher-
ents. So why shouldn't they all peacefully coexist, just as

widely different works of modern art coexist in the art gallery?

The Californian, *very* Californian, philosopher of science Paul Feyerabend (1975) argued in this vein for what he called an "anarchistic theory of knowledge"—by which he meant, he really did mean, *scientific* knowledge. Neither philosophers nor any others are entitled to stipulate in advance what is going to be allowed to count as genuine scientific method, or where the boundary between science and nonscience is to be drawn, or anything else of that sort. Any attempt to lay down rules in advance only invites transgression—as everyone knows in the case of art, but as is also true in the case of religion and (according to Feyerabend) even in the case of science. Haven't there been lots of historical examples of extremely distinguished asses trying to rule out in advance as counterintuitive scientific theories such as the transmutation of species, General Relativity, and quantum theory?

Have I made the same mistake in this book? Have I been trying to describe a priori the shape of a future world faith, when on my own antirealist premises the future surely has to be more and more of the sort of formless anarchy that we are already seeing? We have no objective justification for feeling pained by the variety and excess of modern art, and no objective criteria for stepping in and attempting to impose law and order upon it; and by the same token, we surely have no objective justification for feeling pained by the variety and excess of modern religious expression, and no truly objective criteria for stepping in and attempting to impose intellectual order. Why *shouldn't* there be anarchy?

In reply to this important point, I have said three things.

First, we have quite recently emerged from five to seven millennia of agricultural civilization. During this very long period, human life was grounded in a common vision of the cosmic order, and human conduct was guided by laws that emanated from an immensely strong sacred center. We got accustomed to having the moral order and all our values laid on for us: everything was already well founded, familiar, and life was firmly grounded and guided. Now we have suddenly lost all that, and we feel highly disoriented, free-floating.

I have suggested that, at least during the transitional period, we may find it helpful to keep up some of our old and habitual religious practices and attitudes. I have used the phrase the Eye of God for a nonrealistic continuation of the ancient habit of looking at our selves and our own lives as if with a God's-eye view. The old way of living *coram Deo* (as if before the face of God) was valuably consciousness-raising and morally stabilizing, and one may usefully continue to pray to God just as one may find oneself talking to and thinking of a dead person. Secondly, I have used the phrase the Blissful Void for a practice like that of Buddhist meditation or Christian contemplative prayer. We wait in silence for the anxiety-driven rush of language to slow down until we become utterly relaxed. The world unknits itself. We enter a condition of empty void bliss. Is this God; is this absolute nothingness; is this death? It doesn't matter. Nothing matters.

Third, in returning from meditation into active life I have used the phrase Solar Living to describe an expressivist ethic of self-outing, self-outpouring, self-shedding. We are no longer fearful about dying, or afraid to give ourselves away. We pour ourselves out recklessly into symbolic expression and then pass on, pass on, and pass away, without regret.

I have added a fourth theme, the Poetical Theology, meaning that we should regard ourselves as having carte blanche to retell the old stories in new ways. In successive generations, as social values have changed, Hollywood has several times retold the Western myth, injecting new values into it. Indeed, every genre is a myth that undergoes continual revision, and we should support, not condemn as blasphemous, those writers and filmmakers who set out in a similar way to reshape the story of Jesus. Whyever not? There is no such thing as blasphemy.

The fifth theme, World Religion, is the most difficult. I

have prepared the way for it by arguing that: (1) philosophy in the future is going to be completely naturalistic, or this-worldly; (2) in a globalized world we must finally rid ourselves of all those ancient ways of thinking that construct religion by separating in all spheres of life Us from Them, and the Holy from its unclean and excluded Other; and (3) since we have no access to any entirely independent world order or moral order, we should give up the old dogmatic realism and adopt instead an expressivist or "aestheticist" view of the world and of our life.

Although the point is obvious, it remains curiously difficult to recognize that *we made it all up*. We evolved the entire syllabus. We have slowly evolved our own languages, our values, our systems of knowledge, our religions, and our world views. We evolved even our own subjective consciousness, because the brightness, the consciousness, of conscious experience is a by-product of language.

Look out at your own present visual field. What you see before you is in the minutest detail framed and formed by culture and language; framed by cultural categories, seen in the light of theories, formed by words, colored by our feelings and evaluations. Our world is our own self-objectification.

We see around us the accumulated product, the "objectivity," of our own history. Language reflects the point. For example, *France* is the name both of a people and of the land and the cultural tradition, the social world, which that people have established around themselves. A person's native land, her home, her family, her *oeuvre*, her world, is her "objectivity," the accumulated product of her self-expressive life activity with others. Insofar as my world, my objectivity, is beautiful, I rejoice to pour out my life and die into it; insofar as it is ugly, unjust, and despoiled, it is a judgment upon me and my life, and I must strive to mend it.

Against this background, we can see what a World Religion might be. It follows from the new post-Kantian, post-Romantic vision of the self as being not a spiritual substance purifying itself for eternity but a solar process pouring itself out into symbolic expression in its world. Get in the way of seeing your visual field as your own work of art, and you will understand the point. Astoundingly, environmental ethics and postmodern spirituality turn out in the end to coincide. Our spiritual life, our quest for redemption, and our world-building activity all turn out to be the same thing. There really *is* an intimate relationship between psychology and cosmology, our inwardness and our objectivity, microcosm and macrocosm.

In the long term, then, we want religion to become a unifying expressive activity through which we can simultaneously get ourselves together and build our common world. But it would be wrong to close without mentioning the short-term problem: What are we to do in the meanwhile?

Until quite recently the human world was divided into half a dozen principal culture areas, each with its own long-established religious vocabulary. Now, quite suddenly, culture is becoming fully globalized; but we do not yet have any global religious vocabulary. Until one develops, how is the individual religious person to get by?

In the short term, it is best to continue to practice one's own local and traditional faith, but on a *strictly* nonrealistic or consistently demythologized basis. Thus, many members of Sea of Faith (religious radicals; see chapter 12) believe in a nonrealist reading of Christianity, somewhat as follows:

1. God is the "religious ideal"—that is, a unifying symbol of our common values and of the goal of the religious life.

2. The God of Christians is love—that is, the Christian specification of the religious ideal makes agapeic (disinterested, or "solar") love the highest value.

3. We see love as taking human form in Jesus—in the stories told by and about him, and in the various doctrinal

and other stories that have subsequently developed around him.

This minimalist version of Christian theology derives from the great German Protestant tradition of Kant and the Ritschlians. It offers a basis on which one can continue to be a Christian (of sorts) without having to profess any untrue or irrational beliefs.

Other faiths too can be, and are being, practiced in a similar interim way. But it is even more important that we should begin work without delay on the development of a new world faith.

The account I have been offering recently (1994, 1995*a*, 1995*b*) describes the philosophical core of a new world religion as a new way of feeling and living our own relationship to the world of our common experience:

> Empty yourself out over the world through your eyes, as a painter does. Feel how world-energies come welling up and support you, and in return language flows out from you to form, organise, make conscious and embellish the world of your experience. From moment to moment, in our own life-activity, the world pours out. [1995*b*, p. 19]

An obvious difficulty arises. Not only is this entirely novel kind of religion very difficult to explain, but also one may find that even close friends and allies are unable to recognize it as religion.

Confronted by this difficulty, one may be tempted to conclude that no entirely new framing or conceptualization of religion can hope to be understood until the decay of the old faiths has gone much further than it has yet.

I don't agree. I think that we must hurry. Unless something new is launched quickly, I fear that the process of post-modernization will have gone so far, and will have become so destructive, that it will be too late.

ⲉBIBLIOGRAPHY

Akizuki, Ryomin. 1990. *New Mahayana: Buddhism for a Post-Modern World.* Trans. James W. Heisig and Paul L. Swanson. Berkeley, Calif.: Asian Humanities Press.

Armstrong, A. H., and R. A. Markus. 1960. *Christian Faith and Greek Philosophy.* London: Darton, Longman and Todd.

Augustine. 1945. *The City of God.* Trans. by Sir Ernest Barker. Everyman's Library, 2 vols. London: Dent; New York: Dutton.

Banton, Michael, ed. 1966. *Anthropological Approaches to the Study of Religion.* London and New York: Tavistock Publications.

Barthes, Roland. *Mythologies.* Paris: Editions du Seuil, 1957; Eng. trans., New York: Hill and Wang, 1962.

Bloch, Maurice. 1992. *Prey into Hunter: The Politics of Religious Experience.* Cambridge: Cambridge University Press.

Bloom, Harold. 1991. *The Book of J.* Trans. from the Hebrew by David Rosenberg, interpreted by Harold Bloom. London: Faber.

Burke, Peter. 1992. *History and Social Theory.* Cambridge: Polity Press.

Carter, Robert E., ed. 1990. *God, the Self and Nothingness: Reflections Eastern and Western.* New York: Paragon House.

Cassirer, Ernst. 1944. *An Essay on Man.* New Haven: Yale University Press.

————. 1946. *Language and Myth*. New York: Harper.

Cochrane, C. N. 1943. *Christianity and Classical Culture*. Oxford: Oxford University Press.

Collingwood, R. G. 1940. *An Essay on Metaphysics*. Oxford: Oxford University Press.

Corrington, Robert S. 1994. *Ecstatic Naturalism: Signs of the World*. Bloomington: Indiana University Press.

Cupitt, Don. 1980, reissued 1993. *Taking Leave of God*. London: SCM Press.

————. *The Sea of Faith*. London: BBC Publications, 1984; 2d ed. rev., SCM Press, 1994.

————. 1994. *After All: Religion Without Alienation*. London: SCM Press.

————. 1995a. *Solar Ethics*. London: SCM Press.

————. 1995b. *The Last Philosophy*. London: SCM Press.

de Burgh, W. G. 1923. *The Legacy of the Ancient World*. London: Macdonald.

Eliade, Mircea. 1954. *The Myth of the Eternal Return*. New York: Bollingen Foundation and Pantheon Books.

Evans, G. R. 1993. *Philosophy and Theology in the Middle Ages*. London: Routledge.

Evans-Pritchard, E. E. 1956. *Nuer Religion*. Oxford: Oxford University Press.

Feyerabend, Paul. 1975. *Against Method: Outline of an Archistic Theory of Knowledge*. Atlantic Highlands, N.J.: Humanities Press; reprinted, London: Verso Editions and New York: Shocken Books, 1978.

Foucault, Michel, *et al.* 1988. *Technologies of the Self*. London: Tavistock.

Freeman, Anthony. 1993. *God in Us: A Case for Christian Humanism*. London: SCM Press.

Geering, L. G. 1980. *Faith's New Age*. London: Collins.

————. 1994. *Tomorrow's God*. Wellington, N.Z.: Bridget Williams Books.

Gillespie, Michael Allen. 1995. *Nihilism Before Nietzsche*. Chicago: University of Chicago Press.

Goodman, Nelson. 1978. *Ways of Worldmaking*. Indianapolis: Hacket Publishing.

Guthrie, Stewart Elliott. 1993. *Faces in the Clouds: A New Theory of Religion.* New York: Oxford University Press.

Hamilton, Malcolm. 1995. *The Sociology of Religion: Theoretical and Comparative Perspectives.* London and New York: Routledge.

Harland, Richard. 1987. *Superstructuralism.* London: Methuen.

Harvey, David. 1989. *The Condition of Postmodernity.* Oxford: Blackwell.

Heidegger, Martin. 1987. *An Introduction to Metaphysics.* Trans. Ralph Mannheim. New Haven: Yale University Press.

Hick, John. 1989. *An Interpretation of Religion.* London: Macmillan.

Hinnells, John R., ed. 1985. *A Handbook of Living Religions.* London and New York: Penguin.

Hocking, W. E. 1932. *Re-thinking Missions.* New York: Harper and Row.

Horton, Robin. 1970. "African Traditional Thought and Western Science." In *Rationality.* Ed. Bryan R. Wilson. Oxford: Blackwell, pp. 131–71.

Jacobsen, Thorkild. 1976. *The Treasures of Darkness: A History of Mesopotamian Religion.* New Haven and London: Yale University Press.

Jung, C. G. 1954. *Answer to Job.* Trans. R. F. C. Hull. London: Routledge and Kegan Paul.

Kandinsky, Wassily. 1977. *Concerning the Spiritual in Art.* Trans. M. T. H. Sadler. New York: Dover Publications.

Kant, I. 1987. *Critique of Judgment.* Trans. Werner S. Pluhar. Indianapolis: Hackett Publishing.

Karim, Wazir-Jahan. 1981. *Ma'Betisék Concepts of Living Things.* London: Athlone Press.

Kaufman, Gordon D. 1975. *An Essay on Theological Method.* Atlanta: Scholars Press.

———. 1993. *In Face of Mystery: A Constructive Theology.* Cambridge, Mass.: Harvard University Press.

Kelly, C. F. 1977. *Meister Eckhart on Divine Knowledge.* New Haven: Yale University Press.

Keppel, Gilles. 1994. *The Revenge of God: The Resurgence of Judaism, Christianity and Islam in the Modern World.* Trans. Alan Braley. Cambridge: Polity Press.

Kierkegaard, Soren. 1941. *Concluding Unscientific Postscript.* Trans. David F. Swenson and Walter Lowrie. Princeton, N.J.: Princeton University Press.

———. 1962. *Works of Love.* Trans. Howard and Edna Hong. London: Collins.

Kraemer, Hendrik. 1938. *The Christian Message in a Non-Christian World.* New York: Harper and Row.

Kroker, Arthur, and David Cook. 1988. *The Post-Modern Scene: Excremental Culture and Hyperaesthetics.* London: Macmillan.

Lecercle, Jean-Jacques. 1985. *Philosophy Through the Looking-Glass: Language, Nonsense, Desire.* London: Hutchinson.

Lessa, William A., and Evon Z. Vogt. 1958; 3d ed. 1972. *Reader in Comparative Religion: An Anthropological Approach.* New York: Harper.

Lévi-Strauss, Claude. 1973. *Totemism.* Trans. Rodney Needham. Harmondsworth, U.K.: Penguin.

Lindbeck, George. 1984. *The Nature of Doctrine: Religion and Theology in a Postliberal Age.* Philadelphia: Westminster Press; London: SPCK.

Ling, Trevor. 1968. *A History of Religion East and West.* London: Macmillan.

Megill, Allen. 1985. *Prophets of Extremity: Nietzsche, Heidegger, Foucault, Derrida.* Berkeley: University of California Press.

Miles, Jack. 1995. *God: A Biography.* London: Simon & Schuster.

Moorey, P. R. S. 1987. *The Ancient Near East.* Oxford: Ashmolean Museum.

Morris, Brian. 1987. *Anthropological Studies of Religion.* Cambridge: Cambridge University Press.

Murdoch, Iris. 1966. *The Time of the Angels.* London: Chatto and Windus.

Murray, James A. H. Beg. 1888. *A New English Dictionary on Historical Principles.* Vol. 1. Oxford: Oxford University Press.

Niebuhr, H. Richard. 1952. *Christ and Culture.* London: Faber and Faber.

Nietzsche, Friedrich. 1968. *The Will to Power.* Ed. Walter Kaufmann. New York: Vintage Books.

———. 1968. *The Twilight of the Idols* and *The Anti-Christ.* Trans. R. J. Hollingdale. New York: Penguin Books.

Otto, Rudolf. 1925. *The Idea of the Holy*. Trans. John W. Harvey. Oxford: Oxford University Press.

Parker, T. H. L. 1975. *John Calvin: A Biography*. London: J. M. Dent.

Parry, J. H. 1949. *Europe and a Wider World, 1415–1715*. London: Hutchinson University Library.

Phillips, D. Z. 1993. *Wittgenstein and Religion*. London: Macmillan.

Phillips, J. R. S. 1988. *The Medieval Expansion of Europe*. Oxford: Oxford University Press.

de Polignac, François. 1995. *Cults, Territory, and the Origins of the Greek City-State*. Trans. Janet Lloyd. Chicago: University of Chicago Press.

Pritchard, J. B. 1969. *Ancient Near-Eastern Texts Relating to the Old Testament*. 3d ed. Princeton, N.J.: Princeton University Press.

Renfrew, Colin. 1987. *Archaeology and Language: The Puzzle of Indo-European Origins*. London: Jonathan Cape.

———, and Ezra B. W. Zubrow, eds. 1994. *The Ancient Mind: Elements of Cognitive Archaeology*. Cambridge: Cambridge University Press.

Rorty, Richard. 1982. *Consequences of Pragmatism*. Brighton, U.K.: Harvester Press.

———. 1991. *Essays on Heidegger and Others: Philosophical Papers, Vol. 2*. Cambridge: Cambridge University Press.

Sandars, N. K. 1972. *The Epic of Gilgamesh: An English Version with an Introduction*. London: Penguin, rev. ed.

Serres, Michel. 1995. *Angels: A Modern Myth*. Paris and New York: Flammarion.

Smart, Ninian. 1989. *The World's Religions*. Cambridge: Cambridge University Press.

Smith, W. Cantwell. 1963. *The Meaning and End of Religion*. London and New York: Macmillan.

Stark, R., and W. Bainbridge. 1987. *A Theory of Religion*. New York: Lang.

Sutherland, Stewart R. 1984. *God, Jesus and Belief*. Oxford: Blackwell.

Sutherland, Stewart, Leslie Houlden, Peter Clarke, and Friedhelm Hardy, eds. 1988. *The World's Religions*. London: Routledge.

Taylor, Mark C. 1992a. "Reframing Postmodernisms." In *Shadow of Spirit: Postmodernism and Religion*. Ed. Philippa Berry and Andrew Wernick. London and New York: Routledge.

————. 1992b. *Disfiguring: Art, Architecture, Religion*. Chicago: University of Chicago Press.

Tillich, Paul. 1951. *The Protestant Era*. London: Nisbet.

————. 1987. *Visionary Science: A Translation of Tillich's "On the Idea of a Theology of Culture."* With an Interpretive Essay by Victor Nuovo. Detroit: Wayne State University Press.

Tylor, Edward B. 1871, in 2 vols. *Primitive Culture*. London: John Murray.

Urmson, J. O. 1990. *The Greek Philosophical Vocabulary*. London: Duckworth.

Ward, Keith. 1994. *Religion and Revelation*. Oxford: Clarendon Press.

≡INDEX